WE CAN ALL DO BETTER

WE CAN ALL DO BETTER

——•——

BILL BRADLEY

 Vanguard Press
A Member of the Perseus Books Group

Published by Vanguard Press,
A Member of the Perseus Books Group

Books published by Vanguard Press are available at special discounts for bulk purchases in the United States by corporations, institutions, and other organizations. For more information, please contact the Special Markets Department at the Perseus Books Group, 2300 Chestnut Street, Suite 200, Philadelphia, PA 19103, or call (800) 810-4145, extension 5000, or e-mail special.markets @perseusbooks.com.

Editorial production by Lori Hobkirk at the Book Factory.

Cataloging-in-Publication Data is available at the Library of Congress
ISBN 978-1-59315-729-6—ISBN 978-1-59315-730-2 (e-book)

10 9 8 7 6 5 4 3 2 1

For my daughter

Contents

Introduction

For eighteen years, I was a U.S. senator. Then for three years, I ran for president. For the past twelve years, the equivalent of two Senate terms, I've worked in finance, including venture capital, investment banking, and money management. People ask me what I miss about being in politics. The answer is twofold: I miss concerning myself with public policy seven days a week and interacting with constituents. For me, American democracy is, as Woodrow Wilson put it, a "sacred mystery."

I was always moved by the special relationship between a legislator and his constituents. In my Senate days, I would travel around New Jersey, my adopted state, trying to capture in my mind and heart the essence of the New Jerseyness I sought to represent. I believed I had been elected to use my judgment, not to be a weathervane swiveling in whatever direction the popular wind pointed. But that still meant I had an obligation to listen to my constituents before I voted.

Next to a large canvas sign reading "Meet Senator Bradley," I would stand in the concourse of the Port Authority bus terminal, where ten thousand New Jersey commuters rushed past in an hour, my hand outstretched, my aides ready with pen and paper in case someone's question required more information than I could convey in a fleeting moment. I would walk the beaches of the Jersey Shore, each summer covering the hundred and twenty-seven miles from Cape May to Sandy Hook, in what I called a walking town meeting; moving along the high-water line, I would answer questions, shake hands, catch Frisbees, pose for photos, and generally enjoy myself. At local Democratic Party events—dances, dinners, cocktail parties—I would heed the advice an old pro once gave me, "Billy, you got to kiss the women," only to come home at night drenched in the aromas of a hundred different perfumes.

New Jerseyans, like most people, cared about the big issues: jobs, health care, education, the environment, pensions, along with issues of foreign policy that bore on our national security. They were interested, too, in purely local issues: airport noise, commuter trains, road construction, and beach replenishment. I would stand before three hundred people in a town hall, taking their questions and gauging their moods—and I would ask myself, "What made these three hundred people come out on this freezing winter (or rainy spring) night to ask me questions?" Sometimes the answer was simple curiosity, but usually they wanted to find out whether they agreed with my views on the economy, foreign policy, or a hundred other issues. Sometimes they just wanted to have their say. I found the job of being their senator a big, exhausting, and wonderful responsibility.

I was frequently rejuvenated by these interactions with constituents. Occasionally I was their piñata, but most often they shared their concerns and hopes with me. They told me how they were coping and what they thought government should do and not do.

They asked me to help them with a mistake made by the federal bureaucracy—a lost Social Security check, an immigration problem. Their very presence at a town meeting or issue forum, their visits to my offices in New Jersey or Washington, DC, was testimony to their faith in our system of governance. They saw that the system was theirs.

The mystery for me was the connection I felt to them. I had always been curious about other people and enriched by their stories. But there had to be more to it than that. No one in my family had ever held elective office. My father, the local banker, was treasurer of the school board in our hometown of Crystal City, Missouri, for over twenty years, and my mother was a fourth-grade teacher and later a volunteer in church and civic groups. Both parents drilled into me, by word and example, the value of altruism, of giving a part of yourself to another human being. In a family like mine, idealism came naturally, but politics was another matter. My father wanted me to be a gentleman, my mother wanted me to be a success, but neither wanted me to be a politician.

But there was something moving and powerful to me even then about a group of citizens interacting in the knowledge that their collective opinion could have an impact. Democracy, I came to realize, worked only if people assumed their responsibility as citizens. If they didn't act, the monied interests controlled the process. If they took the initiative, our history showed that they could change the country's direction.

Whenever I go back to that small town that sits on the west bank of the Mississippi, I go down to the river and stand for a while, watching it flow. It scours half a continent on its way to the Gulf of Mexico, and I imagine it all starting with one drop of water that with other drops forms a trickle that becomes a branch that flows into a creek that feeds into a river that flows into another, larger river, and another, and another, until there it is before me—the mighty Mississippi. In those moments, the river is, for me, a metaphor for our democracy. Both start with a single, small, seemingly insignificant thing—one drop of water and one citizen—that comes together with others and still others until you have a powerful current that sweeps away anything in its path. That river best expresses the mystery of democracy for me. "Out of many—one," it says on the dollar bill. That's true of a river and a democracy.

I look at our world as it is today and wonder how our American story will evolve. There are so many uncertainties, so much division, so much pain, yet I also see unlimited potential. The question is, Can we make the decisions now that will secure us a better tomorrow?

Sometimes in a democracy there is a standoff between two irreconcilable points of view. This was the case in the years leading up to the Civil War. Short of resorting to violence, you resolve such conflicts with political combat that, though vicious, is bloodless—until one side wins. Even given our current political paralysis, I don't believe that America is fundamentally different today than from years past. But our specific circumstances are indeed different, and our margin for error is much less. Will one party crush the other, or will we get together across party lines? Or will the emergence of a new party be the catalyst that allows us to act decisively before our economic crisis reaches the tipping point, destroying our common welfare and diminishing our power in the world?

We are confronted with many pressing social issues, but the issues critical to our nation's future relate to our economy, our foreign policy, and our political system. What follows is my attempt as a citizen to grapple with those challenges. By focusing on them, I necessarily leave out other important areas—pensions, health care, and the environment among them. Our economic challenges are complex, so when I write about the economy there will be a lot of numbers. I don't want to oversimplify. People must understand the totality of what we face so that they can make their choice about what kind of country we will become. I hope to lay out what we must do in the short, medium, and long term to raise the standard of living for all our citizens. I intend to suggest an approach to foreign policy that, while it might seem new, is really as old as the country. Neither of these programs is likely to be achieved without changing our politics, with its corrosive influence of money and ideology. All of this is offered from the perspective of one whose active political life is over but whose love of country will never die.

These pages were largely inspired by a passage in Lincoln's second State of the Union address, in which he said, "We can succeed only by concert. It is not 'Can any of us imagine better?' but 'Can we all do better?'" That is a question for us as a nation and for each of us individually. Can we all do better? The relevance of Lincoln's question to the fragility and inequality of our economy, the direction of our foreign policy, and the paralysis that afflicts our national dialogue is indisputable. The challenges we face require all of us to be at our best. Yet our fate as individuals, even at our best, is tied to the success of our national community. No one of us is an island, even in a country as big as America. Larger forces—a flood, a hurricane, a financial crash—can overwhelm us as individuals, but together we can prevail. We learned that early, as Americans: The pioneers were courageous individuals who acted in concert to raise their neighbors' barns and bring in the harvest. Only by banding together did we secure our independence, settle a continent, win our wars. The challenges before us in our nation's third century are no less stark.

"Can we all do better?"

1

The Context

The social, economic, and fiscal problems the country now faces are severe and challenging in fundamental ways, and all of us must be willing to be part of the solution. The job will be difficult. The present powers-that-be are formidable. Those who would change our country must have vision and courage.

There are answers to our problems. They require will, discipline, and sacrifice to bring about, but even that is not sufficient. As citizens, we must have the confidence that our democracy gives us the tools to improve our circumstances. As human beings, we must see our interconnectedness and recognize that we are capable of great things when we cooperate with one another. These attitudes are necessary because the problems we face come from neglect over many years—by both of our major political parties and by ourselves as individual citizens. Just as no one guaranteed that the Greek, Roman, or Ottoman empires would last forever, no one has guaranteed America its continued dominance in the world. If overreaching abroad and decay at home cause us to falter, the world will be a place with considerably less hope.

America's idealism, optimism, and spirit of self-reliance, its cele-bration of concerted action, its suspicion of the abstract, its hands-on practicality, its recognition that in hard times people need one another—all these have created the unique American character, a character that has inspired people around the globe. But the Amer-ica of today is in a state of confusion. We don't see our problems clearly; or if we do, we often—out of inertia, fear, or greed—fail to deal with them. We too frequently live in the past or revel in the present instead of adopting the actions that would secure the future. The federal government has amassed an enormous debt in just the last ten years. Many of our state and local governments, far from being laboratories of democracy, have pursued the "free lunch," spending lavishly on pensions and health care and then handing on the bill to future state administrations. Much of the financial sector seems unable to decide whether it wants to help build a new world or suck the life out of the declining one. The corporate sector is con-sumed with the short term, trapped in a financial prison of stock buybacks and quarterly earnings reports, unable to invest or hire in its own long-term interest. Ten years ago, sixty-one U.S. companies had triple-A bond ratings; today there are four. Our culture also seems excessively coarse, marked by gratuitous violence and sex without meaning. Everywhere people are making excuses for their failures, from the athletic field to the corporate boardroom, and then salving their mistakes in the warm balm of public relations. As long as you act a hair's width within your lawyer's definitions of the law, you get a pass that exempts you from doing what is not just legal but also right.

I had a friend who worked at the highest levels in three major investment banks over twenty-five years. He told me that once when he refused to work on a deal because he didn't think it was right, the head of the firm came to him and said, "I know what we're doing is unethical, even immoral, but I can assure you it's not illegal." The travails of our major religious institutions—the Catholic Church with its pedophilia scandals and cover-ups; the gay-bashing fundamentalist preachers arrested on morals charges; the four rabbis in New Jersey convicted in 2010 of money laundering—serve to remind us that while no one is free from sin, the land is engulfed by arrogance, hypocrisy, and self-righteousness. Meanwhile, secularists indiscriminately deplore the spiritual bedrock of every society since the time of the ancients.

Exacerbating these failings is a mass media that champions the superficial, sensational, and extreme view. Style, social trends, sports, and popular culture are often covered in greater detail than foreign and economic policy. Only a few major newspapers, all of them under relentless financial pressure and apparently unable to reinvent themselves in order to attain a level of profitability, still attempt to ferret out the truth, but reporting, the craft of going out to discover what isn't known, too often gives way to opinion pieces. Paying serious television journalists good salaries costs more than putting two guests on the air with a celebrity host to bat around some issue without reference to the facts. The guests spin the issue to suit their interest, and the host, given the pressure of time, often doesn't follow up. These exercises rarely educate or even try to persuade the audience with facts and analysis; rather, they tend simply to confirm knee-jerk opinions. Thanks to demographic targeting, a TV network knows what the viewers of particular programs care about—what appeals to their tastes and moves them to action—and playing to these preconceived ideas ensures a high Nielsen rating and consequent healthy advertising revenues. Fox News Channel is one of the most profitable news organizations in the world.

The losers here are the people, who would like to know: What happened in the city council meeting? Or in the congressional committee room? How was the money for schools spent? How did that special-interest tax break make it into the tax code? Who agreed to the pensions that bankrupted our town? What did corporation X do for the ten thousand workers it just fired? How will the latest technological innovation affect jobs? These are the kinds of questions that rarely get answered, at least on television. If people in power are not held responsible for what they do, it will be easier for them to abuse that power. Without facts to challenge a government official or a CEO, the people's questions and accusations are parried by elementary public-relations tactics.

It's a sad comment on the media that it is rewarded more for invading the privacy of celebrities—even, as we saw in England last summer, hacking their cell phones—than for uncovering fraud in the defense sector or revealing the misuse of union members' dues. Instead of investigating a politician's private life, the media should be investigating his or her public actions. There's a Pulitzer Prize embedded in nearly every tax or appropriation bill if a journalist simply digs for it. Would the pure food and drug laws have passed, or even have been proposed, in the early twentieth century without the muckrakers? Would Watergate have led to Nixon's resignation without the *Washington Post*? Would the Vietnam War have become as controversial without TV network reporting in the war zone?

Now the military has learned how to handle the media, too, by confining the information flow to the briefing room, so that what's seen on TV is not the war itself but what some general wants us to know about the war. Corporations have departments devoted to crisis management, so that when an embarrassing story breaks, the danger can be contained by admitting wrongdoing to some lesser offense and promising quick action to punish a few low-level perpetrators. If the story is about an investigation, the suggestion for the accused is always to settle as quickly as possible. When the press charges you with a cover-up, you just release mountains of information, which gives the appearance of transparency and guarantees that the press will generally fail to uncover the buried incriminating information.

Occupants of the White House in recent administrations have played the game of manipulation as well as any CEO, and often more ruthlessly. If you become a relentless questioner, you'll be estranged from the White House. What journalist would want to be cut out of the flow of leaked information? Your editors will wonder why you aren't getting the good stories. Your family needs your paycheck, so you tone down your intensity and settle for covering the dueling press releases of two candidates, or two legislative parties, with the full knowledge that objective truth is the casualty. Moreover, the twenty-four-hour news cycle is relentless. With two to three stories breaking every day, often planted by campaign consultants, reporting in depth on the country's real problems becomes difficult. With this kind of media culture, is it any wonder that we know less and less about what's going on around the globe?

The current American condition exists in a world where other nations are on the rise: China, with 1.3 billion people, a relentless work ethic, strong families, economic farsightedness, and a thirst for higher living standards; India, with nearly 1.2 billion people, a burgeoning entrepreneurial drive, deep spiritual traditions, and a functioning democracy; Brazil, with plentiful water, rich forests, farmlands, mineral wealth, and a developing sense of democratic nationhood; Indonesia, with abundant natural resources, a presence on both sides of the Malacca Straits, and a unique cultural mix of animism, Hinduism, Buddhism, and Islam; Turkey, with a history of empire, a unique position between Europe and Asia, and relative stability in a volatile part of the world. And as America confronts new ambitious national actors, it must still cope with such mature powers as Japan, with its democratic rule of law, technological prowess, and highly educated population; Russia, with its massive mineral and energy reserves and renewed strategic assertiveness; Europe, with its euro zone market (bigger than our own), its diverse talents, and lessons learned from a bloody history; and finally our neighbors to the north and south, Canada and Mexico—one remarkably stable, the other threatened by the flow of drugs north and guns south—without whose friendship our world would be a much more dangerous place.

This is not 1945, when the United States bestrode the world like a Colossus. Today our circumstances are more perilous than in the past. The full-time job of leadership requires more subtlety. Listening carefully to partners and opponents alike is as important as impassioned oratory. Persuasion is the leader's most effective tool and national example his best weapon. We need to foster a new spirit of partnership among all countries, in which we learn from what other societies have to teach us as diligently as we promote our homegrown solutions.

Our international standing will diminish unless we get into shape—not just in the next administration or the next decade or the next big crisis, but now. In fact, the crisis is here today; it is a slow-motion crisis. Our predicament is like that of the frog in the pot of water on the stove, who doesn't notice the temperature is rising until it's too late. You see denial of reality in everything from our eroding infrastructure to our declining dollar. Timidity and self-interest have produced the bad public policy that has gotten us to this point. And time is running out. We're lucky that the financial crash of 2008–2009 woke us up to an aspect of our situation and offered us a window into what has gone wrong. Can we marshal the willpower, discipline, candor, imagination, and resilience to bounce back from where the last several decades have put us? Can we regain our championship form?

America starts with many strengths. We are endowed with vast natural resources. Our economy is still the largest and most dynamic in the world by a wide margin, with the most sophisticated capital markets and the most mobile population. Our people are resourceful. Our graduate schools and many of our universities are among the best in the world. Our political institutions remain flexible enough to accommodate bad news and then allow us to regroup. We have a legal system that functions with relative impartiality (unless you're poor and black) and a judiciary that for the most part is above politics. Americans remain deeply patriotic, willing to heed the nation's call in times of danger. An appealing tolerance allows most of us to live side by side with people from different backgrounds in such a way that we often learn from them. Creativity abounds—from scientific research to the arts, from entrepreneurship to the innovative cultures of many large business organizations.

Americans, although we differ on the best way to respond to it, are uncomfortable with the poverty in our midst. It offends our sense of America's promise. Most families teach their children to be diligent and abide by the rules, because they believe that with honesty, hard work, and a little luck you can accomplish anything in America. The nonprofit sector has given the charitable impulse a way to improve society and has provided individuals with the means to serve their neighbors. History itself gives us reason to hope—from the revolution led by George Washington to the efforts in nation building by Jefferson, Adams, and Hamilton to the leveling instincts of Andrew Jackson, the almost mystical sense of destiny expressed by Abraham Lincoln, the tough progressivism of Teddy Roosevelt and Woodrow Wilson, the ebullient canniness and resolute courage of FDR, the plainspoken decisiveness of Harry Truman, the battle-tested wisdom of Eisenhower, the expansive inclusiveness of LBJ, the unflagging determination of Ronald Reagan. The outcome of upheavals in each of these presidents' times was uncertain. Settling a continent, fighting a civil war, overcoming the violence and inequality of industrialization, persevering through world wars and ideological confrontation, rebounding from economic depression after economic depression, overcoming the legacy of slavery, and remaking our democracy at regular intervals: America has been tested. Each time the challenge seemed formidable. Each time we made it through. The assumption is that we will make it through our current crisis, too, but nothing is guaranteed. In a democracy, it depends on what the people want and how their leaders lead.

In times of great stress, inaction is not an option. You have to act, because if you don't change the downward trajectory of a bad situation it will only get worse. Wishing it weren't so doesn't make it better. Ignoring it perpetuates it. Only well-considered action will allow us to move beyond our current situation.

Can we all do better?

2

Members of the Club

On a cold night in early November 2008, two hundred thousand people assembled in Chicago's Grant Park. Giant television screens had been placed at strategic points on the lawn. There was an air of exuberance and anticipation. All eyes were on the stage with its colorful backdrop and long runway, where any moment now Barack Obama would emerge to speak for the first time as president-elect of the United States.

The joy was palpable, all across the country. More than 70 million of our fellow citizens gathered around their television sets. Something historic had happened. Whether you were black or white or Hispanic or Asian or whatever—if you had lived in America over the last fifty years, you had seen the slow decline of racial strife. The election had confirmed that movement in our collective humanity. But this night was about more than race, or how yet another person from humble origins had ascended to America's highest office, or how the young president-elect had beaten the political odds to win the nomination. It was about a new generation of Americans discovering their inspiration in the words of a political leader, and an older generation finding those words more deeply imbedded in their souls than they would ever have thought possible. Barack Obama convinced us that we could change our country, that one person could make a difference, that a new set of possibilities for ourselves, the country, the world was emerging.

One month earlier, in the midst of the presidential campaign, the stock market had cratered and the financial system had almost collapsed. Pension funds plummeted overnight, and job loss soon followed. Americans were afraid—aware that we were reaping the consequences of years of economic mismanagement. The country needed to believe in itself again. And the world needed to believe that the United States hadn't forgotten its historic role as an engine of hope and example of justice.

With his family at his side, Barack Obama took the stage. The applause was thunderous. Grown white men cried openly. Jesse Jackson stood on the lawn, wiping tears from his eyes. Young Americans screamed their lungs out. People around the world were watching, rapt at what was happening in America that night. TV commentators let the moment speak for itself. Oprah Winfrey put her head on the shoulder of a stranger in the Grant Park crowd and sobbed, overcome by the moment. The president-elect kissed his wife and his two girls, stepped forward, and said,

> If there is anyone out there who still doubts that America is a place where all things are possible; who still wonders if the dream of our founders is alive in our time; who still questions the power of our democracy, tonight is your answer.
>
> It's the answer told by lines that stretched around schools and churches in numbers this nation has never seen; by people who waited three hours and four hours, many for the very first

time in their lives, because they believed that this time must be different; that their voice could be that difference. . . .

It's the answer that led those who have been told for so long by so many to be cynical, and fearful, and doubtful of what we can achieve to put their hands on the arc of history and bend it once more toward the hope of a better day. . . . Tonight we proved once more that the true strength of our nation comes not from the might of our arms or the scale of our wealth but from the enduring power of our ideals: democracy, liberty, opportunity, and unyielding hope.

For that is the true genius of America—that America can change. Our union can be perfected. And what we have already achieved gives us hope for what we can and must achieve tomorrow.

In the next day's *New York Times*, Ethan Bronner, writing from Gaza, declared, "From far away, this is how it looks: There is a country out there where tens of millions of white Christians, voting freely, select as their leader a black man of modest origin, the son of a Muslim. There is a place on Earth—call it America—where such a thing happens."

When Obama was elected, he came to office as the personification of hope and the realization of the American dream, having established through two years of campaigning a unique bond with the American people. The honeymoon would not last long. Six days later, Lawrence Downes of the *New York Times* wrote, "It's time to pack away the Obama glow. Young people should save it for when they're old. The men who landed at Normandy spent no time thinking about what an awesome invasion they had just pulled off; they had to go liberate Europe. Postgame celebration and analysis are fine, for a game, but this country's challenges are not recreational." Within three weeks, ratings for cable news and news websites had

dropped precipitously, and news leaks from the presidential transition effort had mushroomed. Within six months of Obama's inauguration, the momentum, based on a carefully crafted story the
nation believed in, dissipated as the reality of Washington took hold.
Many of Obama's newly assembled team of advisers seemed more
comfortable with the tribal rituals of the capital than with the aspirations of the country. The president was gradually deprived of the
oxygen a politician needs—his encounters with the people—and he
appeared to be listening to those who told him what he couldn't do,
instead of those who told him what he'd been elected to do.

Disgust with the federal government—particularly the Congress—
has never been higher. In a late September 2011 *New York Times*/CBS
poll, only 6 percent of respondents—an all-time record—believed
Congress deserved re-election. President Obama's approval rating
hit a low of 40 percent in the October Gallup Poll. The fact that we
seemed unable to get our economy growing again and that American
troops were at war on the other side of the globe had something to do
with those numbers, but so did the nation's perception of the culture
of Washington, driven by that city's obsessions: power and money.

Most members of the Washington insiders' club come to town
brimming with idealism, and then something happens. It's as if there
were something in the air there that changes them with every breath.
Lawyers rarely graduate from law school with dreams of becoming a
lobbyist, but if you're a lawyer in Washington, that's where the action
is. Most political consultants begin their careers in a campaign that
stirs their souls, and then they get hooked on the adrenalin of combat
and the money from lucrative consulting contracts. Pundits often
start out as journalists and then morph into opinion-spouting television celebrities. Think-tank stalwarts get caught up in a swirl of fund-
raising and media strategies that leave little time for their substantive
work. All these "members of the club" love their country. They work

hard at building their professional skills. They love their friends and their families. They have dreams for their children. But when it comes to politics, most of them can't break free from the cynicism that dominates the Washington culture and snuffs out the quintessentially American can-do spirit.

High-tech detective agencies investigate the most personal aspects of politicians' or appointees' lives. Members of administrations settle internal disputes by leaking their versions of an event or their opinions of a colleague, and the media turn the gossip into news, because it's easier to report on people than on policy. Rumors spread like wildfire. The press arrogates to itself the right to see if a politician can "take a punch," even if it's below the belt. Today, in a culture whose main rule is "last man standing," politics is mean and virtually everyone is a pitiless critic.

During my eighteen years in the U.S. Senate, I saw the Washington knives come out on more than a few occasions. George H. W. Bush, an honorable and talented president, won the first Gulf War, reduced the deficit, resolved the savings-and-loan crisis, passed a strong clean-air law, signed the Americans with Disabilities Act, and deftly presided over the end of the Cold War—yet he failed to win a second term. The press helped to bring him down from a post–Gulf War approval rating of 89 percent by ridiculing him for such trivialities as a distaste for broccoli and not knowing what a supermarket barcode was, a lapse intended to show that he was out of touch with middle-class families—as if any president would (or should) do the grocery shopping for the White House. When he reversed his promise not to increase taxes ("Read my lips!"), the media treated it as a sign of inconsistency and weakness, not as an act of courage by a political leader willing to change his position because the needs of the country demanded it. Bill Clinton read the tea leaves and shrewdly took advantage of that widespread depiction.

For the lobbyist members of the Washington club, government power can be an aphrodisiac. The best calling card in today's Washington is to be a friend of the president. The next best is to be a friend of the committee chairman or the cabinet secretary. Lobbyists love to use their connections—to exercise them for their clients. The amount of money that changes hands in some of these transactions is mind-boggling.

Many members of the club treat even the smallest disagreement as if it were a blood sport. Witness two consultants of opposing parties blasting each other on a talk show in order to prove their aggressive bona fides and drum up business. Pundits hold forth on TV with ironclad certainty (Washington is not the place for nuance), and when whatever they so confidently predicted does not come to pass, few hold them accountable. Members of the Washington club exude a smugness based on the premise that they've been around and they know how things work: Big dreams—idealistic dreams— cannot be realized. They've seen politicians come and go, and their views are etched in stone: "Reagan will never make it; he's just an actor." "Hillary Clinton's the inevitable Democratic nominee." "You can never reform the income-tax code." "You can never pass major health-insurance reform." Then there is the current conventional wisdom, which hasn't been disproved . . . yet: "You'll never be able to raise taxes or substantially reduce the deficit." And "The two parties have a lock on politics."

Politicians tend to tell people what they think people want to hear. They spout bromides and hurl vitriol at one another on TV. Twenty percent of their supporters cheer: "Way to go! No compromise!" But the 80 percent sitting at home and watching these spectacles is appalled. The hostility, the rigidity, is foreign to their own experience. On the Sunday talk shows, administration spokesmen rely on poll-tested phrases, and the opposition counters with poll-tested rhetoric of its own. Compare those shows with the stories about real people's everyday lives carried on CBS *Sunday Morning* and you'll see the difference between posturing and reality. One show reveals the true America, the other the trivial nation of the permanent political class.

If the Washington culture is cynical, its most frequent expression is complaint. No president, at least since I went to Washington in 1979, has ever measured up for members of the club, no matter what his ranking in the polls. At nearly every reception or dinner party, you learn that there is something wrong with the president, whoever he is: "The president isn't reaching out properly." "He doesn't have strong command of substance." "He's too cocky." "He needs more backbone." "His cabinet is mediocre." "He seems isolated." "He should be more sensitive to human needs." Or more this and less that. The state of perpetual dissatisfaction is not a state from which dreams can spring. If you're a politician, the Washington club is the hammer and you're the nail. The unspoken premise of many media interviews is that you are probably not telling the truth. Few in the club are moved by honest sentiment or devotion to public service. Most see everyone in politics as attempting to manipulate everyone else. Politics, they believe, is all about posturing and self-interest. The electorate, they think, is uninformed, the politicians venal. A politician's expression of emotion is invariably disbelieved and often ridiculed. The admission that you don't know something is seen as weakness. The sad irony is that many members of the club may be idealists underneath, for as the saying goes, a cynic is nothing more than a disappointed romantic.

Contrast this picture with the way most people in America live their lives. Even as their economic prospects have declined in the last thirty years, they have continued to believe in their country's fundamental health.[1] They give their neighbor the benefit of the doubt. They look for silver linings. They take selfless actions. They make due. They endure.

When I ran for the Democratic presidential nomination in 2000, my conviction about the decency of the American people was only amplified. They wanted to believe in a positive future. They looked to you with the expectation that if you were president you could change their lives for the better. To be worthy of that trust, you gave them the best you had, you answered all their questions, you responded to the problems they confronted, the dreams they held onto, the frustrations they felt. A great deal of respect was conveyed—not so much for me as for the office I aspired to, which is why it is such a tremendous privilege to place yourself before the citizens of this country and seek the presidency.

Some of the people I encountered, to be sure, were unreasonable, angry zealots. The great majority were not. You would stand before an audience, with all eyes on you. I loved the eyes, in which I could read doubt or hope or anxiety or anger or support. I loved connecting with people in the audience until you had the whole room going with you as you tried to persuade them of your views. Most Americans will give you a hearing if they sense that you're putting the country ahead of your party and telling them the truth. I enjoyed sharing stories from my life and my hopes for the country. I especially enjoyed listening to their stories, which were full of unexpected twists, sometimes sad, occasionally funny, and frequently inspirational. When you are a politician who tries to feel the heartbeat of your district, or your state, or your country, you get a sense of the whole, a feel for what binds us together as citizens. The knowledge that hope is still alive outside our nation's capital balances the cynicism of the club and reminds us of what we have done and can do again.

3

Breaking the Logjam

The economic crisis confronting America requires action in the public and private sectors alike. We face a deterioration of the middle-class standard of living, a weakened economy that needs to be stimulated (even if that temporarily increases the cyclical deficit), and an unsustainable long-term deficit driven by inadequate tax revenues and explosive entitlement spending. To deal effectively with the crisis, we need a three-part strategy: immediate, proximate, and long-term.

The State of the Economy

In 2008–2009, in response to the worst financial collapse since the 1930s, the federal government used its economic tools to keep the nation out of a depression. The Federal Reserve injected a massive amount of liquidity into the economy so that banks could resume lending and businesses could resume hiring, creating three times as

much money in one year as it had since it came into existence. In
addition, the Congress passed a $700 billion bailout of banks and a
$787 billion spending bill, most of which stretched over 2009 and
2010. Still, unemployment remained above 9 percent. Might it have
gone to 11 percent without the stimulus? No one really knows. President Obama chose to go with what he thought he could get. In ret-
rospect, it appears that the stimulus should have been bigger. If we
had done as much as China did with its 2009 stimulus as a percent
of GDP, ours would have been $1.9 trillion. The lesson is clear. China
has bounced back from the downturn. We're still stuck in it.

In the hope of getting the economy moving again and people
back to work, the Congress passed a bipartisan lame-duck tax agreement in December 2010. The bill kept income tax rates at their current level until 2013, reduced employee Social Security taxes by a
third to 4.2 percent for one year, and extended unemployment benefits through the end of 2011. The result is unclear: Unemployment
hasn't budged much, but the bill did increase the deficit by $450 bil-
lion per year.

Even though 58 percent of Americans thought the stimulus
would work, according to a *Washington Post–ABC News* poll taken
shortly after its passage, that confidence in Washington is gone.
Only 26 percent of the people believed Washington could solve the
country's economic problems, according to another *Washington Post–
ABC News* poll, in August 2011. There are several explanations for
the growing unease: In November 2011, according to the Bureau of
Labor Statistics, nearly 22 million Americans who wanted full-time
jobs couldn't find them. Banks still aren't lending to small businesses;
housing is still flat on its back. But the relentless attack on the stimulus by Republicans has also played a role. People see Washington
irrevocably divided into two warring camps that care more about
political advantage than about the country.

A New America Foundation study in October 2011 by Daniel
Alpert of Westwood Capital, Robert Hockett of Cornell, and Nouriel
Roubini of New York University points out that since the 1980s the
entry of 2 billion low-wage workers into the world economy from
high-savings, export-oriented economies like China and India has
produced an excess supply of labor in the world. Asian economies,
remembering the lesson of the 1997–1998 financial crisis in which
they were caught with inadequate currency reserves, have built up
substantial holdings of dollar assets and other currencies, leading to
another excess supply—a glut of capital. Instead of spending that
money to generate economic growth for their citizens, they're putting
it away for a rainy day. Global production capacity now exceeds demand by a sizable margin. There are too many sellers and not enough
buyers. Currency wars are not impossible. Given the financial volatility and general uncertainty of our times, business investment isn't fill-
ing the gap. These factors, combined with the dramatic increases in
productivity driven by information technology, the development of
global supply chains, and the erosion of organized labor's bargaining
power in the private sector have led to stagnant wages in the United
States and a growing income inequality that has only been accentu-
ated by the high return on capital at the expense of labor over the
last fifteen years. A world burdened with an over supply of capital and
labor is not a world of rapid economic growth.

The sizable monetary and fiscal stimulus of 2008–2010 has not
produced a sustainable economic recovery. The intractability of
today's unemployment is worrisome. The time gap between losing a
job and getting another one is now over forty weeks—the highest it's
ever been.[1] Houses bought over the past decade and a half are unlikely to regain the pre-bust prices anytime soon, and banks exposed
to these declining asset values and rising default rates will remain
vulnerable, unlikely to lend much more for years. The economists

Carmen Reinhart and Kenneth Rogoff, in their 2009 book *This Time Is Different: Eight Centuries of Financial Folly*, point out that "major banking crises take four to five years to work out and raise government debt levels by about 80 percent over pre-existing levels." The recent bursting of the credit-fueled asset bubble is that kind of crisis. This is not your normal recession.

The deteriorating economy manifests itself in people's everyday lives. Tim Cook, pastor at the Church of Conscious Harmony in Austin, Texas, reflects on his own journey: "In my first post-college decade, I had a good job and made good money. I had a company car, an expense account, and great credit that I learned how to leverage to maximize the cash flow. I owned a home and was accumulating assets. My debts did not seem like a problem because I learned how to keep refinancing them in order to have sufficient cash to be financially free to do all the things I loved doing and to have all the things I loved having. I worried about money constantly, but I never really saw it as a problem because I could always get more of it . . . until I lost my job. Suddenly, I had no cash flow and huge debts . . . I filed for unemployment benefits and began to receive $135 per week to live on. To my great shame, humiliation, and embarrassment, collection agencies began phoning me at all hours of the day and night. I sold everything I could, including furniture, just to try to keep the house."[2] Tim Cook's story is familiar to millions of Americans who can't find a job. The details take the dry unemployment statistics to another, more compelling level.

Jobs, Housing, and Infrastructure

No modern president has ever been re-elected with the unemployment rate above 7.2 percent. It will take large, targeted action to get unemployment below that level anytime soon. Putting money in people's pockets by cutting their taxes makes sense only if that money gets spent, thereby increasing demand for goods and services and stimulating job creation. Most of the cut in Social Security taxes will not be spent on consumption in a world where people fear being laid off, housing prices have plummeted, and nearly one in four Americans with mortgages owe the bank more than their home is worth. Most people will use the money to pay down debt or simply put it aside as savings.

When it comes to proposed federal action to create jobs, every dollar spent in the current environment of declining confidence in government should go to the establishment of a specific job; people have to see the connection between their tax dollars and job creation. Our economic pundits often fail to consider that in a democracy people have to be brought along. The times require a more direct approach. When a government's credibility has been damaged for whatever reason, it cannot shrink from boldness. It must act in a big way to generate more jobs with a short-term, mid-term, and long-term strategy.

The President should announce a short-term program whereby, if company X is employing five hundred people and chooses over the next year to hire thirty additional employees (without laying anyone off), the federal government will pay 30 percent of the cost of hiring the new workers, up to a maximum of $25,000 per worker per year for two years. Companies would not simply be taking the government's money; since they'd have to pay 70 percent of the cost, they wouldn't hire unless they were certain that an additional worker would add to their productivity. The two-year program would be capped at $50 billion per year, and the subsidy would be granted on a first-come, first-served basis, thereby encouraging immediate hiring. If enough employers respond to the program, unemployment could drop dramatically; an average $15,000 subsidy per job would create over 3 million jobs. If no companies stepped forward, there would be no cost to taxpayers—so not one federal dollar would be spent without creating a job. The net cost would actually be below $50 billion per year, because as people went to work they would no longer receive unemployment benefits and they would pay higher taxes. Lower unemployment delivers a lower federal deficit.

The political value of this proposal stems from its clarity. An unemployed worker, his future employer, and voters can understand what the government is doing to create a new job. It is paying 30 percent of the costs, making it easier to hire more workers. Economists suggest cutting taxes, but it's not clear to most people how that will create jobs, because the government has no direct tie to the new job. If President Obama were to propose such a large subsidy and the Republicans were to reject it, even with over 8 percent unemployment, he would win on an issue that 82 percent of Americans say is a top priority.[3] If Republicans, on the other hand, agreed to the proposal (since it does benefit Republican employers), unemployment would drop and America would be stronger.

The President should also immediately do something about housing, which continues to drop in value. In February 2011, housing starts hit one of their lowest levels since 1946, when record-keeping began. In the short term, the quickest and easiest course would be to refinance all government-backed mortgages at 4 percent, today's typical fixed thirty-year mortgage rate.[4] The total amount of mortgages with interest rates at 4.5 percent or above held by Freddie Mac and Fannie Mae, the two quasi-governmental mortgage guarantors, is $2.4 trillion. Refinancing them could save homeowners an estimated $85 billion per year.[5] Such refinancing would reduce defaults but not increase the deficit, and some of that $85 billion could find its way into either additional personal spending, higher savings, or lower debt burdens. Fannie and Freddie might have lower income and asset values, but the country would be better off.

There are other helpful ideas to reduce foreclosures. Creditors can be encouraged to refinance a home at its current market value, thereby giving the hard-pressed owner a reduced monthly payment and the bank a greater likelihood that it will not have to foreclose on the home. To incentivize banks to refinance mortgage principal, they should be given participation in any capital gain above the new mortgage level. By letting the bank share in any appreciation, the homeowner might be able to stay in his home and still retain some upside potential in an eventual sale. Many borrowers who bought a home they couldn't afford lived in newly built subdivisions and foreclosures have turned the subdivisions into graveyards. In the current economic climate, it is unlikely that any bank will find buyers for the subdivision homes that sit empty, deteriorating rapidly. But rent-to-start-over plans are a solution falling between principal reduction and foreclosure/liquidation. These plans allow people to deed their house back to the bank and get from it in return a five-year market-rate rental contract with payments often lower than the mortgage payments. The former homeowners can buy their house back at any time during the period of the contract, and the bank can sell the house during the same period, but only subject to the terms of the lease.

At the beginning of April 2011, the Federal Reserve reported that U.S. nonfinancial companies had $1.84 trillion in cash and other liquid assets sitting in their treasuries—some of it held offshore. If 20 percent of that were to be spent on hiring new employees at the median U.S. household income level of $49,445, we'd create a minimum of 7 million new jobs and unemployment would drop to under 5 percent. But companies won't hire if they can't sell their goods. It's a chicken/egg situation. When people are out of work, or afraid that the pink slip could arrive any day, they hold back on spending. Because companies can't sell goods, they don't invest and lay off more workers, which only adds to the number of people who don't buy cars, homes, and washing machines. Eventually, home sellers and companies cut prices, but people still don't spend, because they expect that prices will drop further tomorrow. It's a downward spiral. The single most important way to solve our economic problems is to get people back to work, in jobs that have a future. The wealthy don't spend enough to get the economy moving. Only the vast middle class—those Americans making, say, between $30,000 and $120,000 a year—has that power, and public policy for decades has done nothing but deliver them body blows.

To those worried that inflation will result because of the Fed's large-scale money creation and the entitlement spending increases on the horizon, I'd say simply that we're unlikely to experience inflation if consumers and businesses are not spending. And I'd remind those who fear a return of the "stagflation" of the 1970s that even as the economy back then was doing poorly, wages and consumer credit were rising.

Along with the short-term actions related to job subsidies and housing, we need a mid-term approach that will create jobs over the next five to seven years and allow some time, as the New America Foundation study has pointed out, for mortgage holders to work down their debt, U.S. companies to strengthen their positions in international trade, Europe to resolve its sovereign debt and banking issues, China to orient its economy more toward consumption and less toward exports, and the world economy to reduce its excess supply of capital, labor, and productive capacity.

What most people remember about President Franklin Roosevelt's response to the Great Depression are the Works Progress Administration, the Public Works Administration, and the Civilian Conservation Corps, which created jobs for Americans in building schools, parks, roads, dams, bridges. In the small town in Missouri where I grew up, the high school was a PWA project built in 1939. Today, over seventy years later, it stands as testimony to far-sighted government leadership. We need new public investment in public goods that will last another seventy years. To get America back to work, strengthen our national security, and stimulate economic growth, the President should propose a massive nationwide infrastructure-investment program. The New America Foundation study estimates that a $1.2 trillion investment in much-needed infrastructure over a five-year period would generate 5.52 million jobs in each year of the program. There is no other stimulus that could create so many jobs and leave behind a seventy-year foundation for economic growth. Given low interest rates, there will never be a cheaper time to float thirty-year reconstruction bonds. Government-subsidized personal consumption (i.e., tax cuts) in the current climate of debt de-leveraging cannot work; public investment that directly creates jobs can.

Without high-speed rail lines in key U.S. corridors of 750 miles or less—such as Boston to Washington on the Eastern seaboard and San Francisco to San Diego along the Pacific seaboard; the Texas triangle comprising Houston, San Antonio, and Dallas; the Orlando/Tampa/Miami corridor; and the Milwaukee/Chicago/Detroit route—we will become even more dependent than we are now on insecure sources of foreign oil, because people have no convenient mode of transportation except for their cars. Indeed, transportation now accounts for nearly 75 percent of U.S. oil consumption.[6] Without investment in seaports and airports, our points of entry will become increasingly clogged, expensive, inefficient, and even dangerous. Without investment in highways and bridges, we will be less productive and more inconvenienced. These investments interact positively with each other. If high-speed rail connects cities, then airlines can concentrate on longer distances and highways will be less jammed. If airports trade in their old traffic-control technology of the 1960s for what is possible today, delays will fall and productivity will rise.

Just as it did in the nineteenth century, infrastructure investment can lay the foundation for the next wave of economic growth, even as it employs more hardworking Americans. It will also demonstrate to the American people that their tax dollars are being spent on behalf of all of us. In 1987, Ronald Reagan vetoed a transportation bill because it had a hundred earmarked projects. In 2005, George W. Bush, without uttering a word, signed a transportation bill with 6,229 earmarks. Such profligacy may be a good re-election strategy, and it might even employ a few more lobbyists, but it is not a transportation policy. There should be a limited number (under fifty) of projects, and they should be projects of national significance. Each should be costed out rigorously. Individual earmarks must cease; otherwise we'll be wasting dollars with no real national benefit. A 2011 report from the Carnegie Endowment for International Peace by a committee on transportation solvency called for a Transportation Trust Fund that pays for highways, transit and passenger rail programs, and a National Infrastructure Bank—all fully funded, as in most other countries, by revenues from transportation.[7] Specifically, it concluded that to fund infrastructure improvements, we need an oil-import fee that, as oil prices dropped, would morph into a gasoline tax, thus holding the price of gasoline stable.[8] The price of gasoline would rise as the import fee is passed through to the consumer. When the market turns, the consumer will continue paying the former price with gasoline taxes making up the difference, thereby establishing a predictable floor and sending automobile companies the price signal to build more fuel-efficient vehicles. To add urgency to the program, all contractors should be offered completion incentives and asked to put up bonds backing the quality of their work.

Financing Our Debt

Meanwhile, of course, we need to finance our federal debt. Without foreign lenders, that will be difficult to accomplish. Our largest creditor is China, which holds $1.426 trillion in U.S. debt. Many argue that China would never precipitate a financial crisis by selling U.S. Treasury bonds, because such action would mean a drop in the value of the dollar and thus of their remaining dollar investments. They argue also that panic selling of U.S. Treasury debt would hurt the U.S. economy, which in turn would mean reduced exports from China to the United States and thus increased unemployment in China. And then there is the question of where China would put its $3.2 trillion in foreign currency reserves. It seems unlikely that they would buy more yen and give the currency of Japan, their Asian rival, the status of a major reserve currency. The euro is also an unlikely repository. Who knows whether, ten years from now, it will even exist? Currencies such as the Swiss franc or the Singapore dollar or the Norwegian krone don't have enough circulation to be a meaningful alternative for the Chinese. But nations aren't always rational. Our vulnerability is real.

It's wise to remember that those who control the purse strings often control much more. An example: In 1956, the British, French, and Israelis invaded Egypt in an attempt to take over the Suez Canal. At the time, the United States was the world's dominant economy. President Eisenhower was outraged and ordered the U.S. Treasury to start selling the British pound short, thereby putting unbearable downward pressure on that already sinking currency. His administration also prevented the British from drawing down their quota from the International Monetary Fund, further fueling speculation in the pound. Britain got the message and announced its withdrawal within a month.[9] The prospect that China will exert similar pressure on us is not a probability, but it is a possibility. By threatening to sell off our debt or excluding our companies from its market, they might try to influence our actions with regard to Japan, Taiwan, or the South China Sea. Whatever the precipitating event, the faster China's economy grows and the more dollar reserves it accumulates, the more powerful could be such coercive action. Clearly, China is fed up with our failure to deal with our long-term fiscal imbalances. It fears inflation down the road and a depreciating dollar. These concerns make it highly unlikely that China will be at the front of the line to purchase much of the $3.5 trillion in maturing Treasury debt that we have to refinance over the next two years. In January 2011, the Chinese Central Bank ceased to require Chinese companies that earn dollars to return those dollars to the central bank in exchange for yuan; they can now use their dollar earnings any way they want. With fewer dollars at the central bank, the Chinese will be able to say, when we ask them to buy a lot more Treasury bonds, "Sorry, we don't have the dollars to buy more than we already are buying. They're in the coffers of Chinese companies, which, as is the case in your country, we don't control."

Whereas it might be more difficult to count on the Chinese for our government-debt financing, Chinese capital could lay the groundwork for America's next wave of economic growth. If we can control our long-term structural budget deficit, we will need less Chinese investment in Treasury bonds. The Chinese will continue to amass dollars as Americans continue to buy Chinese exports. They could use these surpluses to buy the reconstruction bonds issued by the U.S. government to fund the entire $1.2 trillion in infrastructure investment so critical to the recovery of the U.S. economy. Such action would be a tremendous vote of confidence in our bilateral relationship. We could then use the transportation trust fund for the less high-priority but needed infrastructure improvements. Persuading China not only to fund major infrastructure projects in the United States but also to bring more Chinese companies here to hire Americans (as opposed to simply purchasing American companies) should be another national priority. Japanese investments in the United States since the 1980s have led to the current employment of nearly seven hundred thousand Americans at U.S. affiliates of Japanese companies.[10] More Chinese investment that creates new jobs could provide a win/win way out of our current capital imbalance with China. The British made major investments in the United States in the nineteenth century; it was a good deal for them and a good deal for us. There is no reason, once we act with fiscal prudence, for China not to follow suit in the twenty-first.

Since 1944, when the Bretton Woods monetary system was established, the dollar has been the world's principal reserve currency, which means that many governments hold it as part of their foreign-exchange reserves. Indeed, the dollar represents over 60 percent of the world's foreign-exchange reserves, with the euro next, at 26 percent. For us, the advantage is that the United States can execute international transactions in dollars rather than having to pay the transaction costs of going from one currency to another. With the world's governments holding dollars, it is also easier for the United States to finance its budget deficit. Trillions of dollars need to go someplace. Given the flexibility and perceived advantage the United States has because of its reserve-currency status, China, Russia, and the Gulf Cooperation Council want to replace the dollar with a new reserve system, such as a basket of currencies or special drawing rights issued by the IMF. As a step in that direction, China, Russia, South Africa, Brazil, and India have established lines of credit among themselves in their local currencies. These countries represent a combined GDP approaching that of the United States and more than one third larger in real terms—that is, adjusted for our higher cost of living. Moreover, most of them have a higher growth rate than ours, so they will only become more important over time.

If more countries use dollars only to trade with the United States, gradually the dollar will play less of a role in world commerce. It won't happen tomorrow, but it could happen sooner than you expect. Our economy will reel from the effects of losing our reserve currency status. The government will have to pay higher interest rates to attract the necessary capital for its bonds—or higher taxes to reduce the deficit and therefore our borrowing and exchange-rate costs. There will be less demand for dollars, and the dollar's value will drop. Our imports will then be more expensive. Shortages could develop, as the United States could no longer pay for imports of goods and services with its own paper currency. And we will be unable to replace the imports with domestic production, because we have sent our manufacturing jobs offshore. We'll be just like any other country that consumes more than it produces and borrows more than it saves: We will have to accept a lower standard of living.

Federal and State Budgets

The state of our economy is similar to a turnaround situation in the private sector. When a company is in distress, the CEO decides what to cut, what to consolidate, what to do about pricing, how much additional capital to request, and what to set as the executive team's priorities going forward. He tells all participants that for two years all employees, including himself, will have to tighten their belts and make sure that any expenditure promotes future growth. He lays out a plan and executes it. Today a similar program has to take place in the public sector.

Projecting budget deficits beyond a year or two is difficult. They are subject to assumptions about economic growth and interest rates. Manipulate those assumptions and a deficit projection can be practically anything you'd like it to be. For example, a growth rate 1 percent lower than the projected rate will increase the budget deficit by $40 billion per year, because of lower tax revenues and higher unemployment outlays.[11] In a *Wall Street Journal* opinion piece in June 2011, former Federal Reserve governor Lawrence B. Lindsey warned that if interest rates on government debt return to their levels of the last two decades (5.7 percent per annum, on average), they will add $420 billion in interest costs in 2014 alone. These two unknowns—growth rate and interest rates—make predicting precise budget deficits similar to shooting blindfolded at a moving target. If you try—because Congress now formulates a ten-year budget—to project growth and interest rates a decade out, you enter the realm of fantasy. Inaccurate projections often lead to government policy that exacerbates either inflation by spending too much or recession by spending too little.

Politics will determine whether our long-term structural deficit can be successfully addressed. The structural deficit is the trajectory of spending over current revenues with no changes in law, and it differs from the cyclical deficit, which comes from higher unemployment with its mushrooming unemployment benefits and lower tax revenues. The structural deficit hangs over our future prospects like a dark cloud over the Kansas prairie. Medicare is the starkest example of a federal program with a large structural deficit. That's why actions need to be taken today that will have an effect beginning three to five years from now, when the economy will presumably have recovered. If interest rates remain lower than inflation, the deficit could be reduced over time; the cost of borrowing would be less, and we could repay our loans with the increased taxes arising from inflation. But negative interest rates take a long time to have a substantial effect. Then there are the people who argue for "a little inflation" as the way out of our debt problem, but if the Federal Reserve miscalculates, "a little inflation" becomes much more and the American people pay the cruelest tax of all.

If you want to reduce the deficit without inflation, you have only four areas that will yield significant savings: Social Security, health care (Medicaid/Medicare), defense, and taxes. Cato Institute senior fellow Michael Tanner points out, in *Bankrupt: Entitlements and the Federal Budget,* that if no changes are made in law and if revenues return to their historical level of 18 percent of GDP, by 2050 the big three entitlement programs will consume all the revenue the federal government raises in taxes. In a much closer time frame, by 2015 defense, entitlements and interest on the federal debt will consume 76 percent of the budget.[12] And even after President Obama's healthcare bill fully takes effect, unfunded Medicare liabilities— according to Medicare's trustees report for 2010—will be $28.7 trillion.[13] If we are to pay for such already scheduled spending only with income taxes, then corporate and individual tax rates must dramatically increase; the Congressional Budget Office reports that the top marginal tax rate would have to go from 35 to 88 percent and the 25-percent rate for middle-income workers would have to reach 63 percent.[14] Clearly, the answer doesn't lie in income tax increases alone. Entitlement benefits must also be trimmed, and our national defense must accede to our economic limitations. We should first identify the spending cuts and then increase taxes to pay for the rest of the needed deficit reduction, and pass both the cuts and the taxes in one integrated package, with no loopholes or earmarks or other gifts to members of the Washington club and their clients.

Fifty-five percent of all federal spending is a transfer of money from one group of people to another. For example, we tax workers and send the money to the elderly through Social Security and Medicare, and we tax companies to pay for unemployment compensation. When politicians are unwilling to cut back on these kinds of transfers, what remains to be cut are the government programs that underpin our society: Schools deteriorate; judges and teachers remain underpaid; talented civil servants go elsewhere; needed infrastructure is postponed. An unwillingness to cut the transfers or to close tax loopholes or to raise taxes leads to a country that increasingly will fall apart.

When you consider that state governments, too, have diminished revenue and have made enormous commitments in health care and pensions, you see the full dimensions of the problem. Take the example of courts: Already in some states misdemeanors are ignored. In fourteen states, courts have reduced their hours in session. The courts have been slashed, even as the prison population is growing. The *Economist* recently pointed out that in California, because of budgetary restraints, a typical lawsuit may soon have to wait five years for a trial. The effects of rationed justice abound. As the *Economist* put it,

> The recession left a vast legacy of foreclosures, personal and business bankruptcies, debt-collection and credit-card disputes. In Florida in 2009, according to the Washington Economics Group, the backlog in civil courts is costing the state some $9.8 billion in GDP a year, a staggering achievement for a court system that costs just $1.2 billion in its entirety. To make up the funding shortfall, courts are imposing higher filing fees on litigants. . . .
>
> Even criminal cases are not immune. Some crimes, like domestic violence, have increased with the rotten economy. In Georgia, where court funds have fallen by 25% in the last two years, criminal cases now routinely take more than a year to come to trial. This means that jails are full of the innocent alongside the guilty. Their incarceration adds costs far greater than the alleged savings in the court system. Above all, it causes gross injustice.[15]

I was heartened to hear about Kasim Reed, the mayor of Atlanta, who (like many mayors and governors) inherited an unsustainable pension system that accounted for 20 percent of the city's budget. In nine years, from 2001 to 2009, the unfunded pension liabilities had quintupled to $1.5 billion. Mayor Reed called the union and political leaders in and pointed out that unless they agreed to reductions in pensions the whole system would go bankrupt and no one would have any pension at all. In addition, services would be cut and city workers would be laid off. The city council passed a measure that guaranteed $270 million in pension savings over ten years.[16]

We need more of that kind of candor. Governors in many state-houses have arrived at a moment of truth: No budget gimmick or sleight-of-hand accounting can save them. Selling a few public assets, doing a few one-time fixes, and then passing the buck on to the next governor no longer works. With all the pension and health-care promises, the situation has gotten out of control. City halls will no longer benefit from the deep pockets of fiscally compromised statehouses. The money will begin to dry up, and the mayors will have to break the news to their citizens and admit that they, too, have borrowed to near bankruptcy. They, too, will have to make the cuts or increase the taxes needed to right their ship. The truth is that state and local governments will probably have to do both.

A balanced approach will generate support—if only grudging support. No one wants to have a favorite government program cut back or pay more taxes, but if the alternative is bankruptcy, compromise just might be possible. I cannot emphasize enough the requirement of balance: asking something from everyone. Democrats want the rich to bear the burden; Republicans want to ask primarily the poor to sacrifice. Both political parties champion the middle class and neither asks anything significant of it in this crisis. A true solution cannot give the middle class a pass.

In the early 1980s, Social Security was in danger of going bankrupt. A bipartisan commission composed of respected politicians and economists was asked to recommend measures that would make Social Security secure; the Congress would then vote on those recommendations. As a first-term U.S. senator, I held over a dozen special Social Security meetings in New Jersey to get people's sense of what should happen, given the imperative for some kind of action. At each meeting, I had a professor from the state university explain the exact situation. I then put the options on a blackboard and asked the audience to choose the ones they preferred. The common political wisdom was that the seniors would want tax increases for people paying into the system but not benefit cuts; that workers would want benefit cuts for the elderly and not tax increases for themselves; and that neither the old nor the young would want the retirement age raised. To my surprise I discovered that seniors knew that to save the Social Security system just by increasing taxes would hit their children too hard. They volunteered to take some benefit cuts so the tax increases wouldn't have to be so large. Workers knew that just cutting benefits would hurt their parents, and therefore they accepted some increased taxes. And both groups agreed to raise the retirement age to sixty-seven, if it was done not immediately but over the next several decades. The bipartisan commission recommended all three measures—benefit cuts, tax increases, and raising the retirement age—and the Congress adopted them. The solution asked something of everyone. That's what has to happen today, in the negotiations over our larger budget. And it *will* happen, if the public has anything to say about it.

The Battle over Taxes

Today our politicians tend to score political points by pleasing their most extreme supporters. In last August's Republican presidential debate, one candidate was asked whether he would accept a measure requiring $4 of spending cuts for every $1 of new taxes. He said, "No." How about $10 in cuts for every $1 of tax increase? Again, the answer was no. Finally, the questioner asked all eight candidates, "Is there any ratio of cuts to taxes that you would accept?" and the answer was still no. The exchange revealed an ideological rigidity that endangers America. In a system that requires compromise to advance the public interest, it's difficult to move the country forward if compromise is ruled out. Apparently what was most important to those Republican candidates was the next election, not the economic health of their country.

As we saw in the federal debt-limit confrontation last summer, many Republican senators and representatives seem ready to let the country default on its debt rather than raise taxes. To give you an idea of how radical the views of these latter-day Republicans are, consider Ronald Reagan. He was known by his political base as the president who cut taxes by reducing the top marginal rate in 1981 from 70 percent to 50 percent and in 1986 from 50 percent to 28 percent. What is acknowledged by only a few Republicans, and just as rarely reported by the press, is that in 1982 he presided over the largest peacetime tax increase in American history, which replaced nearly one third of the revenue lost in the 1981 tax cut, and he followed this in 1984 with another large tax increase. He did this by closing a substantial number of tax loopholes—those special exclusions, credits, and deductions that benefit only selected taxpayers. In today's budget debates, the radical Republicans reject loophole closings because they increase taxes on someone. (Actually, closing loopholes doesn't "increase" taxes—it just makes sure that someone who owes taxes doesn't get out of paying them.) By taking this rigid "no tax" position, they forfeit their claim to the legacy of Ronald Reagan.

Before Congress can appropriate money (which means to direct that it be spent), an authorizing committee has to determine the amount allowed for a particular project. The appropriations committee then decides the amount to be actually spent—usually something less than the authorized amount. For tax loopholes, there isn't even an authorizing committee; in effect, it's totally unaccountable spending. Getting loopholes into the tax code is one of the specialties of well-heeled members of the Washington club. That's why a book about the Tax Reform Act of 1986 was entitled *Showdown at Gucci Gulch*, a reference to the hallway, lined with lobbyists, outside the Senate Finance Committee's hearing room. All you have to do in order to cut taxes for, say, corporations that buy a certain kind of machine, or people who buy a house rather than renting, is to stick a loophole in the tax code for them. From a budget standpoint, the result of this kind of tax cut is the same as if it were a spending program: It increases the deficit. You might as well have sent a check from the government to the special interest. Rewarding these taxpayers means that taxpayers who don't exhibit the encouraged behavior (by buying the machine or the house) suffer the consequences of a higher deficit.

There is more than $1.1 trillion of hidden spending in the form of credits, exclusions, and deductions in the present tax code. Most of them benefit some narrow interest—banks, oil companies, real-estate companies, insurance companies, mining companies, and charitable institutions, among others. So the rest of us pay higher taxes than we otherwise would, to make up for the lower taxes levied on the special interests. Russell Long, the chairman of the Finance Committee when I got to the Senate, told me one day, "If you give someone a tax cut, they never remember what you did. If you give them a tax increase, they never forget." Still, politicians believe that the members of the special-interest groups will be appreciative and return the favor in either votes or campaign cash.

The narrower the loophole, the more likely, once it becomes law, that it will remain hidden in the 72,536 pages of the tax code. My favorite story is about the loophole that allows you to rent out your home for up to two weeks and pay no tax on the rent. When I asked how it got into the code, I was told it was the work of Herman Talmadge, the long-serving Georgia senator. Evidently he was petitioned by a few wealthy homeowners near Augusta National Golf Club, which hosts the annual Masters tournament; they wanted to rent out their mansions to other wealthy people who were coming to the Masters. Talmadge accommodated them, and the provision is still in the law. Without a superb tax attorney, no one would know it exists, but the wealthy have superb tax attorneys.

It seems to be a law of nature that whenever you eliminate loopholes, they always seem to return. In 1986, we cut the top individual tax rate from 50 to 28 percent and paid for it by eliminating loopholes used by the wealthy to reduce their taxes, including the exclusion for capital gains. The result was that profits from the sale of capital assets were taxed at the same rates as income from wages. Within months of the Tax Reform Act of 1986 becoming law, lobbyists were advocating for the exclusion's reinstatement. I told them that if they succeeded, the top rate would inevitably rise to pay for it. They were not dissuaded. Capital gains taxes were cut to 20 percent, and the top rate went to 39 percent. The return of loopholes after passage of tax reform is like letting moths get into the closet and chew holes in your brand-new suit.

We can have an income tax system that has lower rates and fewer loopholes and brings in enough revenue for substantial deficit reduction. We can do this by eliminating loopholes and using some of the resulting revenue for a combination of deficit reduction and tax-rate reduction. An alternative approach would be to raise the gasoline tax or institute an oil-import fee, with some of the money going to deficit reduction and some toward income tax or Social Security tax reduction or investment in infrastructure. If you increased the fuel-efficiency standard for cars to fifty miles per gallon, reinstated the cash-for-clunkers program, and phased in a one-dollar gasoline tax increase over ten years, citizens would end up a decade from now paying less for gasoline than they do today.

A third option would be to create a value-added tax and use some of the revenue for deficit reduction and some for credits that would reduce the tax's burden on low- and middle-income people. In an economy where 70 percent of our GDP, in good times and bad, comes from consumption, this tax would guarantee the long-term fiscal health of the United States, just as it has in Canada since 1991.

A fourth alternative would be to cut corporate taxes and raise the top marginal individual income tax rate. This would encourage companies to keep jobs in America and would increase the progressivity of the tax code. In Denmark, for example, the top corporate rate is 25 percent versus our top corporate rate of 35 percent, and the top individual rate is 51.5 percent versus ours at 35 percent. Cutting corporate taxes would make American companies more competitive overnight. I know the CEO of a large multinational company who moved his company abroad to save paying our top corporate tax rate. The company saved $50 million that year, which he kept abroad. "I'd rather pay a lower rate in the United States," he told me, "and use that $50 million to hire U.S. workers."

A final alternative would involve neither income nor consumption taxes. It would tax financial transactions. There are more than 8 billion shares traded daily, largely controlled by computers. If each trade had to pay a minuscule tax, it would raise hundreds of billions of dollars each year to reduce the deficit—caused, in part, let us not forget, by the necessary government spending in the aftermath of the financial meltdown. The rationale here is that those responsible for the financial crisis should pay for its cleanup, while at the same time we would be discouraging the market volatility that works against the small investor—who, in a world of high-frequency algorithmic trading, doesn't have much of a chance on his own.

Have senior citizens so traumatized our politicians that we will never duplicate the achievement of the 1983 National Commission on Social Security Reform? Have politicians become so afraid of the electorate that they won't raise taxes, even on the rich? Are there no broad-based tax increases that the majority of Americans would support? Has the fear of terrorism become so great that we can't cut even those weapon systems and military-force structures that were meant for the Cold War? Are there no additional reforms of Medicare or Medicaid that could lower the trajectory of healthcare spending? The answer to those questions will determine whether we remain perilously vulnerable to the decisions of our foreign creditors or seize control of our own destiny.

In the summer of 2010, *Esquire* magazine convened four former U.S. senators: Republicans Jack Danforth and Bob Packwood, and Democrats Gary Hart and me—all of us colleagues for many years in the Senate. We were given three days in which to balance the federal budget by 2020. Our negotiations were intense, but we did it. The big-ticket items were large defense cuts reflecting our current security needs instead of those of the Cold War; a dollar-per-gallon increase in the gasoline tax, phased in at fourteen cents a year for seven years, along with incentives to increase vehicular fuel-efficiency standards; reduction of most farm subsidies and implementation of a means test for those farmers who make $500,000 or more a year; and reform of the Social Security system by raising the retirement age to seventy by 2057 and changing the way cost-of-living increases are calculated. We improved the current tax code's progressivity by allowing itemized deductions only against the 28-percent rate, and we retained the top rate at 35 percent. Each of us got something in the negotiation. Danforth's major objective was to get agreement that when the budget was balanced, taxes would not exceed 20 percent of GDP (historically they've been 18 percent; today they're at 15 percent). Hart wanted to trim the defense budget of its Cold-War fat. Packwood wanted to keep the top tax rate at 35 percent. I wanted (a) to make the tax code more progressive, (b) to establish an interim disability program for manual laborers if we raised the retirement age for Social Security, (c) to assure a higher miles-per-gallon standard if we raised the gasoline tax, and (d) to avoid any cuts in Obama's healthcare plan. Our interactions resembled the reunion of a string quartet that has played together for many years. Each of us knew how to interpret the others' moves—what was a bluff, what was the bottom line, what each of us said we cared about and what we really cared about. Each of us had to compromise. Each of us knew that without compromise we could not balance the budget by 2020. Our three-day exercise showed that where there is respect and good will, a deal can be struck. Politicians simply need to put country ahead of re-election. The alternative to this course leaves America where it has never been and where no American should ever want it to go—bankruptcy, decline, and rapid loss of world leadership.

The Historical Perspective

For those who wonder what will happen in America given our current political gridlock in the face of truly dangerous economic times, there is no better clue than understanding what happened at other times in history when nations faced large debt issues.

Professor J. Rufus Fears of the University of Oklahoma, a man who has spent a lifetime studying the lessons of history, offers such perspectives.[17] He has drawn some instructive historical parallels to our current debt crisis, pointing out that Plato and Aristotle believed that the very structure of democracies made them fiscally irresponsible. Rome in 70 BCE was a democracy and a superpower, but it had amassed an unsustainable private and public debt. It had an expensive professional army, and its citizens, who had become accustomed to entitlements such as bread and circuses (free food, chariot races, and gladiatorial games), paid no taxes—zero. Provincials provided all the state's revenue. Politicians feared to cut entitlements or impose taxes. Attempts to reduce the debt were thwarted by partisan politics (sound familiar?). It took Julius Caesar to set things right. He solved the private debt crisis by decree: Debtors would pay back the principal they owed but not the interest. He eliminated the public debt by wars of conquest, by an equitable tax system for Roman citizens, and by giving Roman citizenship to the provincials with its attendant tax requirements. The ultimate cost of putting Rome on a sound fiscal footing was an absolute dictatorship.

In 1789, King Louis XVI of France had a gigantic debt problem. He had spent lavishly on his own government, especially its palatial seat at Versailles. Like his predecessors, he had also spent heavily on wars, including the American Revolution. The state's revenues did *not* come from taxing the noblemen or the wealthy merchants. The cost of government was borne by artisans, small businessmen, and even peasants. But Louis needed even more taxes, so he called on Parliament to approve further increases. Instead, the French Revolution began, and he ended up without his head. It was the new National Assembly that had to deal with the French debt. Who would pay taxes? The answer was "Everyone." The assessment of a general tax, however, failed to bring in enough revenue, so the National Assembly confiscated all the Church's lands and used them as assets backing the issuance of government bonds called *assignats*. But the government issued bonds far in excess of the value of the Church's property. The result was inflation, which by 1792 was out of control. Lifetime savings evaporated overnight. The mob took over, and by the time the Terror had ended it is estimated that as many as 40,000 Frenchmen had lost their lives. Still, the fiscal turmoil did not cease. Napoleon stepped in, and France, once again, was governed by an absolute despot. Napoleon, unlike Louis XVI, had a plan for the economy. He backed the currency with gold, taxed all French citizens, embarked on wars of conquest, and (like Caesar, whom Napoleon admired) looted and taxed the conquered.

Now, juxtapose these two historical experiences with the actions of the newly established government of the United States from 1789 to 1791. During the Revolutionary War, enormous debts had been run up by the Continental Congress and the individual states. The states and the congress had paid soldiers in paper money that soon became worthless. The result was a rebellion of former soldiers irate about their circumstances. The unrest and violence in Massachusetts, led by war hero Daniel Shays, alarmed many people, including Washington, Hamilton, and Franklin. It fell to Hamilton, the new treasury secretary, to figure out how to solve the debt problem. Fourteen million dollars was owed to foreign nations, especially France and Holland. The Continental Congress had also sold $42 million in bonds to supporters of the Revolution, both individual Americans and state governments. Finally, the states themselves had issued $25 million in debt.

Hamilton's goal was to establish for the United States a credit rating and reputation for fiscal responsibility as good as those of any European country. The foreign debt was paid in hard currency, backed by gold and silver. The debt of the Continental Congress was paid at the face value of the bonds, notwithstanding the fact that a lot of the bonds were held by speculators who had bought them at a fraction of the face amount, because Hamilton wanted investors to consider future bonds of the federal government rocksolid. The third part of the debt had been accumulated by the states. Thomas Jefferson's Virginia, along with North Carolina and Maryland, because of frugal management had paid off almost all of their debt, and did not want to pay off the debts of such spendthrift states as Massachusetts and South Carolina.

A stalemate ensued, and President Washington told Hamilton and Jefferson to solve the problem. Negotiations bogged down until Hamilton suggested to Jefferson that the capital of the United States be moved to the banks of the Potomac in exchange for Virginia's support of federal payment of state debt. A deal was cut, and the federal government guaranteed the debts of the states. It was because of these decisions that, when the chaos of the French Revolution and the Napoleonic period swept the Continent, Europeans invested readily in U.S. government debt. And when Napoleon decided to sell Louisiana to pay for his European wars, Jefferson could seize the opportunity to more than double the size of the United States, knowing that much of the $15 million could be financed by the rock-solid credit of the U.S. government.

We need look no further than to our Founders for the answer to our current economic crisis and political stalemate. There is often no democratic alternative to political leaders from opposing parties sitting across the table from each other and agreeing on a plan. To do that, you need to know enough about your negotiating partner so that, like Hamilton, you can find the offer that will clinch the deal.

I would say, "Don't count Congress out yet." Good sense and true patriotism may well prevail. Even the staunchest opponents of President Obama are Americans before they are Republicans. I believe they will desist in their vitriol when they see that America is truly at risk without a Grand Bargain encompassing further short-term stimulus and mid-term deficit reductions that include spending cuts and tax increases. So far, that epiphany hasn't occurred. But the prospects of mass unemployment and the stock market crash that could come with it is no gift to the next president, even if he or she is a Republican.

Ideology can drive a country over the cliff. We live at a time when we know what we need to do, but for whatever reason—fear, ambition, ideology—we don't do it. That's the ultimate self-destruction. Let us hope we can meet the challenge without the advent of a Julius Caesar or Napoleon Bonaparte. We're now in uncharted waters. We cannot know whether good sense will prevail. It's our choice.

Can we all do better?

4

Uprooting the Root of All Evil

At the core of the Washington culture is money. It rewards the politically connected. It burdens politicians with the need to raise it. And when they've raised it, it compromises them. The money culture angers taxpayers—it tells them they don't count except as taxpayers who have to bail out banks "too big to fail." It prevents us from breaking the logjam around the deficit. It builds weapons systems unwanted by the military and bridges nobody wants. It protects the old dying industries and ignores pioneering new companies. That kind of money can prevent the best ideas from becoming reality.

In my first campaign for the U.S. Senate, in 1978, I spent a total of $1.68 million for the primary and general election. When Jon Corzine ran in 2000 for the same seat, he spent more than $62 million—most of it his own. The 2008 elections cost a total of $5.3 billion.[1] The 2012 contests could end up costing $6 or $7 billion. The only bright side? Many television stations would not be in business without political advertisements.

Lobbyists know their fields well, and their input to legislation can be valuable, but they should not be allowed to connect the provision of that knowledge with donations of money for a political campaign. There is something fundamentally wrong when a lobbyist—whether representing business or labor—comes to a legislator's office to plead his client's case and then four hours later appears at the legislator's fund-raiser in a nearby restaurant with a $10,000 check. The link between money and policy must be broken.

Obama had a window of opportunity to change our politics. As his first presidential initiative, he could have sought voluntary public financing of congressional and senatorial campaigns. In the early months of his presidency, he had a nearly 70-percent approval rating and a Democratic House and Senate. He could have said that "changing Washington" meant you had to end the money culture. The people had elected him to change Washington, he could have said, and so he wanted hearings on campaign finance reform in the first two weeks of the congressional session and a bill on his desk by March. I believe he would have gotten it, but his political advisors were said to have argued against pushing that reform, because it was not high in the polls on what people really cared about. Of course it wasn't. How could you expect a population in economic shell shock to say anything other than "Deal with the economy, and protect my job and my 401(k), and give me access to health care." The irony is that while reform wasn't high on people's lists, it was absolutely necessary in order to pass laws in the areas that people did list as their top five issues. Without reform, a battle to pass bold legislation on health care or energy or jobs would be a lobbyist's feast, and large-scale success would be diminished— which is what happened.

To anyone who practices politics, the corrupting influence of money seems obvious, but not to the Supreme Court. In 1976, in *Buckley vs. Valeo*, the Court said that the money spent by an individual on his or her own political campaign was political speech, protected under the free-speech clause of the Constitution, and therefore could not be limited. This opened the floodgates for rich people to finance their own efforts. The first thing both parties' campaign committees want to know about prospective candidates is not their biography or whether they have leadership or communication skills but whether they can raise money. By that measure, the best candidate is the one who finances his or her own campaign. According to the Center for Responsive Politics, 250 of our 535 representatives and senators are millionaires.[2] That's 47 percent of Congress. Just 9 percent of Americans are millionaires.[3]

The problem of money in politics is not new, of course. As the vice-presidential candidate in 1900 with William McKinley, Theodore Roosevelt saw firsthand how Mark Hanna, McKinley's campaign manager, required corporations to contribute a percentage of the profits they stood to make from favorable Republican legislation. The practice revolted Roosevelt, who was a true progressive, good-government type. So in 1905, as president, he pressed Congress to ban corporate contributions to political campaigns, which they did in the Tillman Act of 1907. For more than a hundred years it was the law of the land. In 2010, the Supreme Court ruled, in *Citizens United vs. Federal Election Commission*, that the prohibition of corporate contributions for campaign ads was unconstitutional because it limited the free speech of corporations. (One wondered if the Second Amendment, the right to bear arms, would be the next corporate right.) It seems to me that only speech is speech—not money or T-shirts or tents in public parks or whatever. Once you go beyond speech, you are on the slippery slope that leads to arbitrary decisions influenced more by ideology than by common sense. The Court

decisions of 1976 and 2010 have made any comprehensive effort for
campaign finance reform very difficult. All proposals must be voluntary to pass constitutional muster with the Roberts Court.

The reality of politics is so far removed from the Court's decision
in *Citizens United* that you wonder if the Court even understands
how destructive the decision has been to our democracy. It makes
you yearn for justices like President William Howard Taft, Senator
Hugo Black, Senator Sherman Minton, Senator Harold Burton,
and Governor Earl Warren, who actually practiced politics profes-
sionally before being elevated to the Court. They had a feel for
people. They had made mistakes and suffered the electoral consequences. They knew the Court had to work with the world that
existed and nudge it in particular directions. They didn't force their
opinions about what the Founders wanted two hundred years earlier on the America of their day. They knew what it was to compromise and build a coalition. It is, for example, quite conceivable
that only a former politician like Warren—working with three former senators, Black, Minton, and Burton—could have gotten a
unanimous decision on *Brown vs. Board of Education*, the landmark
case that desegregated schools in America.

The Roberts Court is now part of our political money problem,
frequently choosing ideology over common sense, as if its judgments
were divorced from the world around it. Its 2010 decision sits at
the center of the selling of American democracy to the highest bid-
der. Year by year, election by election, decision by decision, power
concentrates in fewer and fewer hands. The interests of the vast
majority of Americans don't seem to be as important to the Roberts
Court as judicial purity. In *Buckley*, the Supreme Court said in effect
that it was just fine that the candidate with little money only has a
megaphone while the candidate with a lot of money has a microphone. In *Citizens United*, the Supreme Court has approved unlimited contributions by super PACs that can steal elections through

widely broadcast lies. Instead of being constructive about a real problem, as Teddy Roosevelt was, the Roberts Court congratulated themselves for adhering to the narrowest interpretation of the Constitution. Today's strict-constructionist justices would do well to heed the words of one of our key Founders, Thomas Jefferson, which is in plain view on the walls of his memorial:

> I am not an advocate for frequent changes in laws and constitutions. But laws and institutions must go hand in hand with the progress of the human mind. As that becomes more developed, more enlightened, as new discoveries are made, new truths discovered and manners and opinions change, with the change of circumstances, institutions must advance also to keep pace with the times. We might as well require a man to wear still the coat which fitted him when a boy as civilized society to remain ever under the regimen of their barbarous ancestors.

Congress is for sale thanks to the Supreme Court's actions, but the situation is even worse than that. Many corporations avoid the disclosure required under *Citizens United*, opting instead to establish 501-C-4 and 501-C-6 nonprofits (often the arms of super PACs), which can spend money on political advocacy without revealing the names of their donors. Some proponents of this scheme go so far as to argue that requiring disclosure would be a violation of First Amendment rights.

In 1998, there were 10,406 registered lobbyists. In the peak year of 2007, there were 14,861.[4] They don't work because of charitable impulses. They serve people who want more money from government, arguing for the passage of laws, regulations, or policy favorable to their clients' enterprises. The economist Mancur Olson argued that the influence of narrow interests can immobilize a democracy and prevent it from addressing the broad public interest.[5] Such influence, like some cancers, grows slowly, but it can be fatal to the efforts by elected representatives to do what the vast majority of Americans need them to do.

There is no place in public policy where the juxtaposition of narrow interest versus general interest is clearer than in tax policy. An ideal income tax system should have the lowest rates for the greatest number of taxpayers and assure that equal incomes are taxed equally and that those who have more pay more. Such a system would have lower rates than the current system and fewer loopholes. We're a long way from that today. Every time regular taxpayers hear about one group or individual getting special treatment, it tells them that government belongs to the few. They're not far from right. Worse, if the special interest gets the tax cut, money that might otherwise have gone toward alleviating the problems of all taxpayers—in big areas such as education, health care, or pensions—isn't there. And because the appetite of the special interest is usually unquenchable, there will be requests for bigger breaks in the future.

Citizens have reason to ask how our democracy works for them. In 1998 the amount spent on lobbying was $1.44 billion; twelve years later the figure was $3.51 billion.[6] In 2009–2010, the financial industry made political contributions of $318 million at the federal level. Healthcare companies contributed $145.7 million. The energy industry gave $75.5 million.[7] Is it any wonder that financial reform was watered down, health care reform had no public option to private insurance, and no energy program became law? Government unions block accountability for the performance of government workers. Congress blocks presidential appointments for the narrowest of reasons, trumping the popular will and rendering government more and more ineffective. To hide the cost of government spending, legislation is rife with special definitions, delayed effective dates, tax breaks extended only for short periods, and rosy economic projections. Laws are passed only to have their effects muted in the regulatory process or their implementation delayed for decades by legal challenges from plaintiffs who hope for repeal by a future administration. All of Washington and most state capitals are in the grip of an insidious kind of corruption—one that uses money and the law to further narrow interests at the expense of the interests of all of us. "It might be unethical, even immoral, but it's not illegal" is the new watchword.

Fannie Mae is the poster child of this kind of legal corruption. It is private in the sense that it issues stock to the public and pays its executives gigantic salaries. It is public in the sense that it was created by Congress in 1938. By purchasing mortgages from banks, which encouraged banks to make long-term mortgage loans, it fulfilled a public purpose. Because the market assumed that the government would back any losses, Fannie Mae was able to raise money at a lower interest rate than private financial institutions. It didn't have to file its financial statements with the SEC, it paid no state or local taxes, it had access to a line of credit of $2.5 billion at treasury, and it was subject only to congressional regulation. These subsidies were giant gifts from the Congress and were ferociously protected by Fannie Mae's lobbying arm. Fannie asserted that all of the cost savings from these government subsidies were used to provide homeowners with lower mortgage rates. The truth was that Fannie kept one-third of the savings (in the billions) for itself, including its highly compensated executives.[8] Whenever a congressman talked of privatizing this behemoth, Fannie rallied its friends in Congress to beat back the attempt. Money was a crucial weapon in its arsenal; between 1989 and 2009 it devoted roughly $100 million to lobbying and political contributions.

Sometimes the most cost-effective investment a company makes is in its Washington office. From 1998 to 2010, when the financial industry bestowed $2 billion on its various champions in Washington, the industry was transformed: Regulation disappeared, leverage increased, risk skyrocketed, and institutions became gargantuan. Each of these steps was made possible by changes in public policy. While the industry's political contributions may be obscenely large, they pale in comparison to the profits made possible by the changes in law and regulation. When the financial industry almost collapsed at the end of that profligate decade, endangering the economic health of hundreds of millions of Americans, lobbyists for the industry went to work on the Hill to make sure that nothing fundamental would change. I'm reminded of a well-meant pep talk I delivered long ago to a high-school student working as a Senate page, which I concluded (perhaps rather patronizingly) with, "Learn how to write an English sentence, know the history and literature of the country. And then with a little luck, you can become a U.S. Senator, too." The page looked at me, puzzled, and replied, "I want to be a lobbyist."

Finance is a little like religion: No one really knows why certain things happen, but we are all deeply convinced of the correctness of our own views. And so here are mine: The financial crisis of 2008–2009 resulted from the interplay of human greed and bad government policy. The former is nothing new; it has been around for as long as we've been on this Earth, and it's what moves markets. But public policy must channel that greed; unchanneled, it leads to disaster. These are what I consider the five public-policy mistakes:

1. *The 1999 repeal of provisions of the Glass–Steagall Act.* In the 1920s, banks took big leveraged risks and lost. The resultant financial calamity set the stage for mass unemployment, home foreclosures, and a decade of human suffering. Policymakers of that era were determined that such a crash should never occur again. They held extensive hearings to understand what had happened, and

they discovered that banks were taking deposits and then speculating with their depositors' money. The Congress decided to prohibit a bank from doing both; it split the old institution into two separate entities. Banks that took depositors' money were called commercial banks, and the government insured their deposits (no more bank runs), but their investments were limited. Banks that didn't take depositors' money became known as investment banks, which in those days were mostly partnerships (each partner had joint and several liability for the firm's finances), and they could speculate as much as they wanted with their own money. The system worked well. Investment banks, because they were investing their own capital, were careful investors. Commercial banks didn't generate large returns, but they were stable. They took in deposits and loaned money out prudently to people who started new businesses, bought homes or cars, bought seed and tractors for the new planting season. The interest these banks paid to depositors was less than the interest they received on their loans, and their profit was this spread. These bankers (my father was one of them) became essential to their local communities.

The arrangement flourished for many years. But by the 1980s, banks had begun to chafe at the limitations of the law. Hadn't floating interest rates on loans and deregulated interest rates on deposits guaranteed the spread for banks and reduced their worry about quality in loans? Why shouldn't commercial banks own insurance companies? Why shouldn't commercial banks make investments for their own benefit and use leverage to turbocharge their returns? Why shouldn't investment banks take deposits, too, and get the federal insurance? How could U.S. banks compete with the big Japanese, German, British, and Swiss banks without these new powers? Bankers maintained that it was ultimately a question of competitiveness. Their lips said it was all about the national interest, but their eyes blazed with dollar signs. When the Glass–Steagall provisions that had reined them in were repealed in 1999, huge integrated financial institutions arose to speculate with depositors' money in relatively unaccountable ways. The share of financial assets held by the ten largest financial institutions went from 10 percent in 1990 to 75 percent twenty years later.[9] All the upside was with the bank. All the downside was with the taxpayer. Heads I win. Tails you lose. The stage had been set for disaster.

2. The failure to regulate derivatives. In the 1990s, executives at the new megabanks found ways to bundle together real assets, like mortgages, slicing and dicing them into new financial instruments that symbolized a real thing but were just numbers on a screen. The daisy chain began with a tangible asset—a house, say, and someone who borrowed money to buy it. The buyer got a mortgage from a bank, which put a thousand such obligations, of varying quality, together into one security and sold it to the public, including other financial institutions. The bank no longer owned these mortgages or bore any responsibility for the loan payments or the mortgages' quality. The investor who bought the security held the risk; the bank became simply a conduit. The derivatives team of the purchasing financial institution then took a thousand of these so-called mortgage-backed securities and packaged them into a financial instrument called a CDO (for "collateralized debt obligation"), which they in turn proceeded to sell to the public and other institutions. This was the second sale of the same asset. But it didn't stop there. A thousand of these CDOs would then be packaged into a CDO-Squared, which was also sold by the latest institutional buyer. The same real asset—a house and its mortgage—had now been sold three times. The financial institutions that packaged each level of derivatives had essentially created money, and the suckers were on the other side of the trade.

Many policymakers and way too many bank CEOs had not the foggiest idea of what was going on. Those who did lacked the strength or vision to call off the party. As Charles O. Prince, the former CEO of Citigroup, said when asked why his corporation bought and sold derivatives, "It bears emphasis that Citi was by no means alone in the view and that everyone, including our risk managers, government regulators and other banks all believed that these securities held virtually no risk."[10]

Finally, to take this process to an absurdity, the daisy chain of selling the same asset over and over was insured by something called a CDS (for "credit default swap"), a kind of insurance that promised to pay someone who bought the CDO if the entities involved couldn't pay them. But this kind of insurance wasn't backed by reserves to assure payment in a crunch. The CDS was nothing more than a fourth sale—all resting on the initial sale of one house. With so much money at stake, the only thing that could rain on the parade was government regulation. So in the last year of his administration, President Bill Clinton signed a law, passed by a Republican Congress, which specifically prohibited the government from regulating the trading of derivatives.

3. *The loosening of regulations for Fannie Mae and Freddie Mac.* It used to be that if you were a president who wanted low-income people to have homes, you had two choices: You could either subsidize their purchase of a home or build housing for them. But in the 1990s, there emerged a third alternative. You could instruct Fannie Mae and Freddie Mac to take on greater risk by investing in subprime mortgages given to people who, by traditional standards, would never have qualified for a loan. The relaxed underwriting standards quickly spread to private lenders, and housing speculation exploded. Prudent capital requirements were jettisoned, and profits soared.

Mortgages were given by banks that never checked the income of applicants. These loans were quickly packaged and sold, and Fannie and Freddie were the biggest purchasers. Their breakdown was only a matter of time.

4. The increase in leverage. This occurred on George W. Bush's watch. In 2004, financial institutions, no longer satisfied with selling the same asset four times, wanted to turbocharge their returns, so they petitioned the Securities & Exchange Commission to allow them to increase what they could borrow for a trade from ten times their capital to thirty or forty times. Warren Buffett has said that leverage is "like driving a car down the road and placing a dagger on the steering wheel pointed at your heart."[11] Everything goes fine until you slam on the brakes. In 2008, the brakes brought the economy to a screeching halt as the speculative frenzy produced a near-death experience for the global economy. Thanks to the government (i.e., taxpayer) underwriting, the dagger didn't reach the heart of the drivers, who were "too big to fail." It was the hapless passengers in the backseat who got hurt— and they didn't even know who was driving the car or how recklessly it was being driven. They just rolled out onto the street to find their houses underwater and their retirement in peril. The quotable Chuck Prince commented about the leveraged lending practices of Citi: "As long as the music is playing, you've got to get up and dance," he told the *Financial Times* back in July 2007. "We're still dancing."[12]

5. The Federal Reserve's demurral. Underlying and abetting the four mistakes listed above was the Fed's ideological view that it had no responsibility for asset inflation, be it a stock market fueled on cheap credit or a housing bubble. Unlike William McChesney Martin Jr., the Fed chairman from 1951 to 1970, who said that his job was to "take away the punch bowl as the party gets going," Alan

Greenspan cheered the party on by keeping interest rates near zero.[13] Who couldn't make money by borrowing at near zero and investing the money in practically anything? And that was before you were permitted to borrow thirty times your capital. Noted financial economist Henry Kaufman likens the proper relationship between the Federal Reserve and banks to that of parent and child: "As guardian, the parents' role is to set out standards of behavior and hold the child to them. A parent should not play the role of friend in his or her relationship with the child. Similarly, the central bank should define and enforce standards of behavior. It should never become a folk hero of the marketplace."[14]

The financial crisis of 2008–2009 was caused by these specific policy blunders, which benefited a few in the financial world, even as they undermined the financial stability essential for economic growth and raising standards of living. Middle-class Americans participated in this fiasco by borrowing money for homes and consumer goods they couldn't afford. But their recklessness was encouraged by liberal credit—and, of course, by the mortgage industry, which gave them mortgages beyond their means because the banks got paid for selling mortgages, not for making sure they were repaid. Besides, the dicey mortgages would probably end up in the coffers of Fannie or Freddie. Your taxpayer dollars at work.

The question asked was never "What is right?" The operative question was "Can I get away with it?" That attitude is symptomatic of the wider cultural norm, which holds that if it's legal, it's OK. If you've ever seen the power of special interests at work in the writing of laws, you know that that's not the right answer.

The Dodd–Frank Wall Street Reform and Consumer Protection Act of 2010 was supposed to prevent another financial meltdown. Instead it risked turning the financial sector into a government monolith. The bill punted on breaking up the too-big-to-fail banks. Far from

it, Dodd—Frank bolstered them against failure and encased the whole
thing in a four-hundred-thousand-word web of complexity that will
serve as a full employment act for many members of the Washington
club. The act provided for an orderly dissolution when a too-big-to-
fail institution got into real trouble. But no one knows how orderly
dissolution will work. As Henry Kaufman pointed out in a speech
to the Foreign Policy Association on December 6, 2011, "Untangling
these credit relationships will affect prices and other market relationships. Who will take the losses? Who will take over the assets and
liabilities as the dissolution proceeds? . . . [A] good portion of the
assets and liabilities will be acquired by other institutions that are
themselves deemed too big to fail. . . . Either way, the entire process
will increase financial concentration." There is only one answer to
this dilemma: Shrink the big financial institutions. You could spin off
the credit-card and consumer-loan divisions into a new company. You
could do the same with the mortgage division or the insurance division. You could even put the investment banking and trading opera-
tion in a new company. After these behemoths have been downsized,
they will no longer be a systemic risk. Small businesses will find easier
financing. Conflicts of interest will end. Large corporations will no
longer receive a privileged flow of funds. The economy will be more
resilient and more stable. The only thing preventing this outcome is
the role of money in politics.

There are ways to keep our sclerotic democracy from succumbing
to the corruption of money. A constitutional amendment, stating
that federal, state, and local governments can limit the total amount
of money spent in a political campaign, should supersede *Buckley*
and *Citizens United*. If that were combined with public financing
for whatever amount was permitted by the campaign finance laws,
we would have returned government to the people. The second way
(either as a part of the constitutional amendment process or in a
freestanding bill) is to establish public financing for all congressional

and senatorial campaigns. For roughly $3 billion a year out of a $3.5 trillion budget, we could shut special interests out of the legislative process entirely, and then legislation would be influenced more by argument and facts than by dollars. Absent the constitutional amendment, a candidate's acceptance of public financing would have to be voluntary. A wealthy candidate, not wishing to limit his spending, could always opt out of receiving public money, but his opponent would be assured enough money to make his case without begging the special interests for it. I know plenty of members of Congress who would rather not spend three hours a day calling strangers for money, but in a catch-22 they're afraid to support public-financing legislation for future elections because this might offend the interests, who then wouldn't contribute to the member's campaign in the pending election. Obama's failure to put campaign finance reform front and center in the first months of his presidency makes it more difficult than ever to achieve today.

Beyond the legislative route to diminish the role of money in politics lies the judicial one. People could flood the courts with cases that take the logic of *Citizens United* to its absurd conclusion. The Supreme Court based its decision on the theory that a corporation is a person—an idea that arose not with our Founders but with the robber barons' court of the late nineteenth century in *Santa Clara County vs. Southern Pacific Railroad Company*, which dealt with the railroad's claim to its right to due process. According to the theory dusted off by the Court in *Citizens United*, a corporation can't be denied its right to free speech since it's legally a person. The absurdity of the ruling is made manifest if one asks, "When was the last time you saw a corporation get married?" or, better yet, "go to jail?" But for corporations there's a downside to being labeled a person. Might the executives of BP, for instance, be charged with murder because, through their position and their neglect, eleven people died in the explosion of the Deepwater Horizon?

When members no longer have to beg for special-interest money, Congress's time could be spent on passing legislation. The reforms I've suggested would build into the structure of politics a force against special-interest deals. When legislators don't have to spend time raising money, they'll have more time to study the issues and talk to their constituents. Evenhanded laws will pass, making America a better country. Politics will once again be a vehicle to improve people's lives—and people will feel the change. Their voices will be heard, online and in person. Their confidence in their own power and their trust in the power of government will grow. And our democracy will be strengthened.

5

Celebrating Selflessness

There's a common conception that human beings are basically selfish. One major political party says that the state must limit the effects of this inherent selfishness through laws and government regulation. The other says that our inherent selfishness can be controlled through the functioning of the free market, which maximizes individual freedom and encourages the rational weighing of costs and benefits, making self-interest mutually advantageous and helping everyone in the long run. What if each of these views proceeded from the wrong assumption—that people are basically selfish? What if, given a choice, most people would prefer to be unselfish—to cooperate, to help others, to work in teams? Might not that new way be the key to our future? One unselfish act is like a large rock tossed into a pond, with the ripples reaching the farthest shore.

In 2004, the president of Sirius Satellite Radio, Scott Greenstein, visited me. Over lunch he explained how disappointed he was by the lack of neutral voices in American politics. The presidential election of that year was just getting under way, and to him it seemed that each side gave the public nothing but spin. Wouldn't it be great, he said, if someone could just tell the public the truth about the vast scope of our problems and what we'd have to do to solve them. Greenstein asked me if I wanted to do that kind of show on his network. I thought for a moment and replied that such a show interested me, but that I'd rather do one that allowed my listeners to hear the kind of stories from people that I'd heard during my forty years on the road, both as a basketball player and a politician. The deeper truth about America lies in the humanity of its people; I didn't want to do just another program on politics. Through the words of Americans themselves, I hoped to present a new perspective on the potential for a government "of, by, and for the people."

The show is called *American Voices* (and I'm happy to say it's still going on). Usually I interview someone who has an unusual job— a boat pilot on the Columbia River, a window washer who works on New York skyscrapers, a groundskeeper at Boston's Fenway Park, a public-health nurse in the Aleutian Islands. Their stories convey the dignity of work, the insights people gain from what they do, and the satisfaction of a job well done. On every show, I also interview someone who is doing something selfless in his or her community. I interviewed Albert Lexie, a man who had shined shoes at the Children's Hospital of Pittsburgh for forty-six years and put a portion of every tip he received into a fund to pay the medical bills of children from poor families. As of the day I interviewed him, he had put more than $100,000 into that fund.

Back when I was running for president, I would often say that this kind of story reflected the goodness of the American people, their generosity, flexibility, and unselfishness. I still believe that. When I began to look in earnest for similar stories for the show, they were easy to find. In fact, they flooded in: There's Carolyn Manning, a woman in Phoenix who collects from local charities the names and addresses of new refugees in her area who have fled oppression somewhere in the world—Bosnia, Iraq, Sudan. Someone from Carolyn's organization, Welcome to America, meets with them to make a list of what they need. Manning then pays them a visit. When the door opens, she says, "Welcome to America," often giving the new arrivals such things as a full set of linens and china. Frequently the families are taken aback. They come from places where the only people you can trust are members of your ethnic group or tribe, never a stranger. Yet here is this woman asking for nothing, just giving. It makes a profound impression. When she says, "Welcome to America," it's not unusual for them to break into tears.

We're a stronger society in the long run if we help those who have fallen on hard times, so they can pick themselves up and move on. On one show, I talked with Thomas Weller, who drives the freeways around San Diego in a souped-up station wagon filled with tires and engine-repair equipment. When he sees people stranded alongside the road, he pulls up and helps them fix their car at no charge. I asked him to tell me about a memorable episode on the road. He said that one day he'd come to a particularly dangerous stretch of freeway and saw a family precariously crowded on the narrow shoulder behind their abandoned car. He pulled over, discovered quickly that they spoke no English, and motioned for them to take shelter behind the pillar of a nearby overpass. He somehow managed to make them understand that he'd come back with his equipment and help them. He returned about thirty minutes later, and when he came around the bend he saw that the family was still huddled behind the pillar but their car, which apparently had been hit by another car, was in flames. "Well, I guess I made a difference that day," he said.

I asked him how he got started driving the roads and helping people. He said that one snowy winter night when he was sixteen and living in Illinois, he was driving alone along a rural road and his car slid off into a snow bank. The motor died and the car was stuck. It got colder and colder. He began to worry. At that moment, a car pulled up. "What's the problem?" the driver asked, and offered to take him to the nearest town, which was fifteen miles away. When the Good Samaritan dropped him off, the boy said he'd like to do something in return, but the stranger wouldn't hear of it. When the boy persisted, he said, "Well, there *is* one thing you can do for me."

"What's that?"

"Pass on the favor."

"So," the patroller of the San Diego freeways told me, "that's what I've tried to do for the past twenty-two years."

Personal experience is life's best teacher. Sometimes it can produce lessons that reverberate out into the larger world. I interviewed Randy Lewis, a Walgreens drugstore executive who ran one of the company's six regional supply centers. Inspired by his autistic son, he asked the Walgreens board for permission to staff 30 percent of his workforce with disabled people. They agreed, and after he had hired people with autism, cerebral palsy, and Down syndrome, he found that productivity improved. For one thing, he said, autistic people do a better job of, say, moving boxes from place to place, because they tend to focus more intensely on repetitive action. What he hadn't expected was the effect that his decision had on the rest of his employees, who were proud of what hiring the disabled said about their company's values.

The 1990 Americans with Disabilities Act removed barriers to disabled people's participation in the daily activities of life, mandating such things as curb ramps, toilet grab bars, and wheelchair lifts on buses. What the act also did was to irrevocably change a national direction. Sometimes after passage of a direction-shifting law it is necessary to aggressively enforce it. (Think civil rights here; the Justice Department filed suits against restaurants that continued to discriminate, or school districts that refused to desegregate.) But after a while, people's values impel them to go further than what the law requires—to its spirit, the dream it embodies. The Walgreens executive didn't need a law: He had his own personal relationship with disability; the law simply created a framework that allowed his request to be taken seriously. In this way, government can encourage people to act from the deeper impulses of love.

Sometimes when we overcome adversity, the experience allows us to find ourselves and guides us to what we really want to do with our life. Molly Barker, a North Carolinian and longtime runner, came from a family with a history of drinking problems. In her twenties and early thirties she seemed headed in the same direction. Then one day at age thirty-two, she went out for a run. She reached a point in the course when her head cleared, and she felt the endorphins flow and the calm descend. After the run, she vowed that she wanted to feel every day, all day, as she had felt on that run. She managed to give up drinking and started a group called Girls on the Run, which aims to show middle-school girls from eight to eleven years old, through running, the spontaneous power they have within, before society can squelch it. In one of Molly's groups was a girl named Brittany. She was mute. She spoke volumes with her eyes and her smile, but never uttered a word. Molly made some inquiries and discovered that Brittany could speak but never did. She had been severely and frequently beaten as a young child. On the last day of the twelve-week course and after each of them had finished a 5K, Molly asked all the girls to describe their experience in Girls on the Run. "Awesome," said one. "Beautiful," said another. "Fun," said another. When it was Brittany's turn, she couldn't say anything. Molly was disappointed.

The next day the group held its appreciation banquet, at which the girls were given various awards. Brittany was called to the stage to get the Grand Communicator Award. As she took the trophy she pulled out a handwritten card and gave it to Molly, who read it to herself and then asked Brittany if she would like to read the card to her teammates. Brittany stepped to the microphone, held the card tightly with both hands, squinched up her eyes and then opened them and looked out at her teammates for what seemed like an eternity. Then she said, "The word I wanted to say on my last day out with Girls on the Run is love." The girls and their families rose in unison and gave her a standing ovation.

When the spirit leads us to take selfless action on behalf of another person, we are expressing our deepest humanity, and that impulse emerges, often, in unforeseen places for unpredictable reasons. I interviewed Linda Bremner, a woman living outside Chicago, whose eleven-year-old son, Andy, had contracted terminal cancer. While Andy was being treated in the hospital, he got a lot of letters from family and friends, but when he came home, the letters stopped. He asked his mother one day, "Mom, have people stopped sending me letters because they know I'm going to die?"

"No, of course not," his mother said. "You'll get more letters, I'm sure." The next day, she started writing him letters signed "A secret pal." If he had a bad week and had to stay home, she'd send him three letters; on a good week, when he attended school, she'd send him one. One night she came into the kitchen and saw him writing something. She tried to look at the piece of paper, but he pulled it away and asked her for an envelope. When she gave it to him, he stuffed his letter into it and asked her to deliver it to his "secret pal." She started to open it, and he said, "No, not you, Mom. Give it to my secret pal." After he'd gone to bed, though, she opened the letter. There was only one sentence. It read, "I love you, Mom."

Several months later, Andy died, and some days after the funeral, while she was doing the painful job of going through his belongings, she found a shoebox on the floor of his bedroom closet. Although he had not been a particularly neat child, she discovered that inside the shoebox were all the letters from his "secret pal," organized chronologically. In the bottom of the box was the address book he'd brought back from the Kids with Cancer camp he'd attended the previous summer. Out of her desire to pay tribute to Andy, she started writing letters to each child in the book, trying to buck them up as she had tried to buck up her own son. An amazing thing happened: She started receiving letters from all over the country asking her to write to another child somewhere who the letter-writer knew had cancer. She honored as many of these requests as she could and finally started a nonprofit organization called Love Letters. In ten years, she wrote over four thousand letters to children with cancer all across the country.

A concerned Sirius executive asked me one day, "What are you going to do when you run out of these kinds of stories?" It's never happened, and it won't, because there are millions of people out there just like the ones I've interviewed. When Americans are moved by something—poverty, homelessness, spousal abuse, failing schools, teenage pregnancy, absence of values, a deteriorating environment—many of them are impelled to do something directly to change the situation for the better. Since the early days of our Republic we have celebrated those who help their neighbors.

When we hear stories about Americans who take selfless actions, we're reminded of what we can do if our heart is big enough, our determination strong enough, and our talent focused enough. There are lessons here for government, too, with its massive resources. If government employees treat their work as just a job, government will fail to realize its potential. The ethos of the nonprofit culture is to give to other people with no expectation of return. The ethos of the private sector is "perform or die." Government is at its best when it combines the selflessness of the nonprofit culture with the accountability of the private sector. That's when it can help to transform the country.

Sometimes a national tragedy calls forth the spirit of our goodness. The greater the need in a crisis, the more we respond to the plight of individuals hard hit by forces beyond their control, and the more we say, "There but for the grace of God go I." A few days after the World Trade Center towers fell on September 11, 2001, I made my way down to the site through streets crowded with the curious and the caring. I remember the stillness south of 14th Street. I remember the pungent odor of the smoldering buildings. I remember the faces of firemen covered by dark-gray dust as they emerged exhausted from looking for survivors in the rubble. Citizens applauded as a fire truck passed slowly down the street. Hundreds lined up outside a large tent that had been set up for pets, hoping they would find their lost dog or cat inside. I remember the messages and photos posted on makeshift bulletin boards around New York by family members hoping that their loved ones were not dead, just missing. Thousands of bouquets were left in appreciation at fire stations across Manhattan. I remember people sincerely thanking policemen, as if realizing for the first time that the police are there to protect us every day.

New Yorkers normally pull together in a crisis—a blackout, a transit strike, a blizzard—but September 11 created a deeper response: People seemed more open, more vulnerable, more interested in their fellow citizens. They prayed together, stood on street corners holding one another. They looked to one another to make sense of what had just happened. And they weren't all New Yorkers or New Jerseyans. Responders came from all fifty states. Oklahoma City EMT workers who remembered digging bodies out of the rubble of their own terrorist event on April 19, 1995, offered the full spectrum of their resources to New York as soon as they heard about the towers falling. Firefighters and EMT workers drove from Long Island and Westchester County, and from Bridgeport, Connecticut; Eureka, Pennsylvania; Brockton, Massachusetts. The tragedy called out the goodness of people in a special way. The target of anger was clear: Al Qaeda. The source of the empathy was more elusive.

At moments filled with collective emotion, hierarchies disappear, ethnic stereotypes fade, the walls of fear and suspicion crumble. What is left is the humanity we have in common. Too often, that humanity is masked by the pursuit of material things, the worrying about what other people think, the grind of events to make an A, to make a living, to move up the ladder. Often we lose sight of our human connection. The challenge is to access every day the energy and empathy that fuels our capacities in a crisis. The result would be the making of a different society—one that the stories of the shoeshine man in Pittsburgh, the welcome lady in Phoenix, the freeway patroller in San Diego, the Walgreens executive in South Carolina, the running coach in North Carolina, and the mother in the Chicago suburbs tell us exists even now, if we simply look around. The citizens who speak on *American Voices* are not all that unusual; they are just in touch with their deeper, altruistic selves—selves that lie in each one of us. That goodness can occasionally be called forth by a leader or by a tragedy, but we will have truly changed our world when we can summon it ourselves every day, in our work and in our lives.

Team Play

A friend of mine, who is a middle-aged female boxer, recently toured boxing programs in East Africa for the World Boxing Council. In the middle of her trip, she sent me the following e-mail:

I look into a young athlete's eyes and I see neither politics, philosophy or religion, just sweat, determination and the joy of the game. A young girl in a burka ushers me into the arena, grasping my arm tightly, because I've come to root for her team. That's who I am to her. Not a Jew, not an American, not an outsider—just a fan . . . and we sit together screaming until our voices disappear.

My friend's e-mail reminded me that sports are universal and carry lessons that can help us reboot our economy. The relationship among members of a winning team offers us a way to think about the connections between ourselves as citizens and what it takes to succeed as a country in the twenty-first century. At some point, it dawns on a member of a team that by helping his teammates he helps himself. Unselfishness begets unselfishness; the result is a stronger whole. Ten years from now, no one will remember who led the NBA in scoring in 2012; they will want to know what team won the championship that year. If you want to be a member of a championship team, you have to care about your teammates. The same is true of our military, whose members are willing to die for their comrades-in-arms. Such fellow-feeling rests in all of us and will emerge if we call on it. We are our brothers' keeper.

Increasingly, businesses find that unselfishness boosts productivity. Five people with different skills, working together as a team, will produce more creatively and efficiently than five people toiling alone in a hierarchy. Harvard law professor Yochai Benkler points out that the Pareto principle—aka the 80:20 rule, and named after Italian economist Vilfredo Pareto—holds that "80 percent of the effort or output comes from 20 percent of the people" and adds that "the best way to get that remaining 20 percent out of the other 80 percent of people is to allow them to contribute small amounts. . . . "[1] Or, as my friend Len Riggio, the Chairman of Barnes & Noble says, "Every human being has a touch of genius. You just have to find it." The 80 percent, in other words, can be valuable members of the team, even if the 20 percent does most of the playing. To some, the guy who sits on the bench doesn't have a role in his team's victory. But the substitute player's effort every day in practice can keep sharp those who do play. His willingness to take a foul, carry the bags, tell a joke, never be late, can also contribute to a winning effort. A grouser can hurt a team, but one who overflows with good spirits can help create a championship atmosphere. We cannot develop our full potential as a country if we don't see that collaborative teams of diverse individuals with hard-earned, unique skills maximize chances for individual success. As Bill Drayton, CEO of Ashoka: Innovators for the Public, and Chairman of Get American Working!, puts it, "This new world will be a global team of teams, teams that come together in varying combinations, scales, and intentions, as the need requires. The faster things change, the more the world will need this giant, fast-moving kaleidoscope of teams. A team is a team only when all its members are players; and in a world defined by escalating change, they can only be players if they can contribute to change."[2]

Major firms increasingly recognize that to foster their employees' talent and loyalty they must not only offer pay and benefit incentives but also take the nonmaterial aspirations of their workers into account. As the Walgreens executive I interviewed discovered, most employees want to see their companies behave admirably. Devising human-relations strategies to promote group solidarity and develop the whole person is in a company's long-term interest. Corporations that promulgate a set of values and care about their reputation for ethical behavior will enhance their success. Or, as Dov Seidman, the chairman and CEO of LRN (a company that helps businesses develop ethical corporate cultures), says: "How a company does things will be as important as what they do." All kinds of companies today seek to make money by doing good. Using the accountability of market thinking and applying it to solve society's problems touches a deep idealism in young people today. Wikipedia, open-source coding of software, and online organizations such as Kiva and Meetup exist because people realize that they can be fulfilled and successful by being unselfish.

Can we all do better?

6

Raising All Boats

One of Americans' bedrock beliefs is in the inevitability of economic progress—the conviction that children will have a higher standard of living than their parents. America has always been a great place to be poor, because someone who is poor today could become prosperous tomorrow. Many real-life examples of people of modest origins becoming rich have embedded themselves in our collective psyche. The belief has been that there is no limit to achievement in America. Anyone can become successful. And success properly has its reward. No one begrudges wealth if everyone is moving up. The key is ambition and hard work—the desire to make something of yourself and the commitment to making it happen.

Upward Mobility

The past thirty years have called this upward mobility into question. The wealth of a very small group of CEOs, Internet investors,

investment bankers, private equity partners, and hedge-fund managers reached mythic proportions. Meanwhile, an alarming number
of Americans continued to struggle to make ends meet. The last
decade in particular has been a lost decade for middle-income families. Median household income adjusted for inflation fell to 1996
levels in September 2010.[1] To maintain even their current income,
middle-class families need two wage earners. In the 1960s, only 12
percent of married women with young children worked; by the late
1990s, that figure had risen to 55 percent.[2] According to the Census
Bureau, in 2010, 46.2 million people lived below the poverty line
($22,350 per year for a family of four)—the highest number in the
fifty-two years that the bureau has published the statistic.[3] (Another
shocking statistic: 27 percent of all African Americans live in
poverty.)[4] The percentage of people living paycheck to paycheck in
August 2011 was 42 percent, according to an annual survey by the
job-search company CareerBuilder. That means 66 million of us live
one pink slip away from economic catastrophe.

Harvard economics professor Lawrence F. Katz offers a clear anal-
ogy of what has happened.

> Think of the American economy as a large apartment block.
> A century ago—even 30 years ago—it was the object of
> envy. But in the last generation, its character has changed.
> The penthouses at the top keep getting larger and larger.
> The apartments in the middle are feeling more and more
> squeezed and the basement has flooded. To round it off, the
> elevator is no longer working. The broken elevator is what
> gets people down the most.[5]

For the next half decade, a large number of Americans face the
prospect of lower wages and fewer benefits, the fear of being laid

off, and lives of much greater insecurity. Ask the insurance accountant who hasn't gotten a real raise in ten years, the airline employee who lost her healthcare coverage when her company merged with another, the call-center operator who lost her job to a counterpart in India, the recent college graduate buried under a mountain of educational debt. Ask the families who can't afford to send their children to college. Ask soldiers who went on the unemployment rolls when they returned from Iraq or Afghanistan. Ask all of them how secure they feel, and the answer would be, "Not all that much." If that kind of insecurity lasts, it will put a damper on our fabled American optimism.

Many American families don't eat out, go to a movie, or take a vacation. They observe a strict budget. Every day is a struggle to survive. They scour the newspaper for coupons that will give them a discount at Walgreens or Target. Some even go dumpster-diving next to the supermarket, looking for day-old bread. They rent living quarters from relatives, cancel the cable TV, plant a garden if they can, use as little as possible of the heat in winter or the air conditioning in summer.

If income has been essentially stagnant, why wasn't there a political explosion years ago? Because we didn't notice. When the income from two jobs wasn't enough, families turned to the home-equity loan, in which you borrow against the value of your house, which in many cases represents your main investment. As housing prices rose beginning in the mid-nineties, millions of people borrowed billions of dollars against the increased equity value in their houses and spent the money on consumption. Since 2007 when the housing bubble broke, the value of homes has dropped, on average, 26.5 percent and more than twice that in some places.[6] In 2010, 23 percent of mortgages were underwater—that is, owners owed more to the bank than their homes were worth.[7] In such a financial tsunami, home-equity loans have screeched to a halt. In 2006, the peak year of housing speculation, banks made home-equity loans and lines of credit totaling $430 billion. After the first nine months of 2009, that figure had dropped to $40 billion.[8]

Americans are cash-constrained and credit-starved. Millions of them feel stuck, plagued with an eerie feeling that neither they nor most likely their children will ever be able to put their feet on the next rung of the economic ladder. Their circumstances generate incredulity and fear. When they look at the seemingly privileged political class, they get angry. When they look at the titans of Wall Street, they go livid.

For thirty years, neither Republicans, who occupied the White House for nineteen of those years, nor Democrats, who occupied it for eleven years, have been able to alter the downdraft in American lives, which has persisted with the exception of a few years in the 1990s. Yet millions of people have seen their taxes go up. Local property taxes have gone up. State taxes have gone up. Social Security and Medicare taxes have gone up. The middle class has been hit hard.

People don't see what they've gotten for their taxes. Roads are deteriorating—just compare a ride from JFK Airport to Manhattan with a ride from the Shanghai airport to the city's Pudong business district. People fear that, even if their sons or daughters do well in high school, college will remain unaffordable. Those without health insurance fear getting sick. Those with health insurance know that many doctors, driven by the requirements of insurance companies, won't give them the time and attention they need. Or they can't find a doctor who accepts Medicare or the health insurance they do happen to have. As for pensions, who can afford to save, with income strained to pay just for living day to day? For years, employees thought they'd have a guaranteed retirement income. Then the company washed its hands of responsibility, ended its defined-benefit plan, and replaced it (if you were lucky) with the contribution of a little money each year into a fund that the employees could invest themselves (whether they had investment experience or not). In 2008–2009, most people with 401(k)s saw their pension assets crater and didn't know where to turn.

Over the last thirty years, companies have come to see eliminating jobs as the first way to cut costs. If a company finds it's cheaper to produce in China, it will just lay off workers. If a company can replace part of its labor force with a machine, it will just lay off workers. If the company has a problem because of a financial crisis, it will just lay off workers. If the company launches a product that the market rejects and the bottom line takes a hit, it will just lay off workers. From the perspective of the private sector, the ease of firing workers gives the United States more economic dynamism. Jobs in uncompetitive companies can shrink quickly, and they can make adjustments and regain their financial health. When labor costs are cut in response to a recession, the downsizing allows the economy to bounce back sooner, and when it does, jobs return. Historically, business cycles worked this way. During the last decade, however, those who were fired didn't find it easy to find another job. Often when they were replaced by foreign labor or by technology, they couldn't get a job with the skills they had developed working for their former employers. A more efficient company just didn't need as many workers. If labor mobility drives economic dynamism and dynamism drives economic growth, then it stands to reason that we shouldn't reduce that dynamism. But, without appropriate public policies, there is a serious human cost to such flexibility.

The frightened, angry middle class of today is an inchoate, unpredictable social force that is up for grabs politically. Its members tend to believe that no one in government understands their real circumstances. They're struggling not to thrive but just to survive. They are fertile ground for demagoguery. The goodness of the American people is still there, but if you're convinced that you've been betrayed by whoever you believe controls the system (the wealthy, corporations, labor, government, bureaucrats, cultural elites, the Washington club), and if you're watching the American dream recede before your eyes, it's easy to turn negative and focus on the greed and incompetence of the powers-that-be.

Long-Term Jobs

The golden age of the American middle class lasted from World War II until the early 1970s. It was based on access to good public education, subsidized home ownership, generous wages and benefits obtained by unions, and a government that kept the leash on the financial sector. The manufacturing sector was the backbone of the middle class. Steel, autos, machines, electrical appliances— Americans knew how to make things (that was one of the reasons we'd won World War II), and the world envied the living standards that such work made possible.

Then competition arose from foreign companies, which didn't have the same labor costs, even though they had workers who were skilled and hardworking. Gradually, manufacturing—everything from glass to machine tools to printed circuit boards—moved abroad, until the number of employees in the manufacturing sector dropped from 25 percent of the labor force in 1970 to 9 percent in 2009.[9] Since 2001, the country has seen over forty thousand factories close and nearly 6 million workers lose their jobs.[10] In addition, there was a multiple of that number lost outside the factory, as supply chains that fed the factories dwindled. People threw their hands up in resignation. We couldn't compete with those labor costs unless we joined in a race to the bottom.

But a funny thing happened. Manufacturing began to have a rebirth. Today it currently represents 11 percent of real GDP, even though we achieve that level with fewer workers. The value of our manufacturing output is greater than China's and increased by nearly one third from 1997 to 2011.[11] Today, our manufacturing is smarter and more efficient, and it is by no means on a downward trend. To the contrary, it is on the upswing. Three hundred and thirty four thousand manufacturing jobs have been created in the last two years—the strongest growth in manufacturing jobs since the late 1990s.[12] Since the low in 2009, manufacturing production has increased 5.7 percent—the fastest pace of growth in a decade.[13]

Cars are still made in America. German, Japanese, and Korean auto companies that have situated their plants here have joined Ford, Chrysler, and GM, employing American workers. Direct foreign investment in America is responsible for two million manufacturing jobs. The German company Siemens has invested $25 billion in the United States in the last decade, employing sixty-four thousand workers across all fifty states. BMW sells cars made in the United States throughout South America. That trend is accelerating, in part because foreign companies want to site their production closer to the largest market in the world and in part because foreign labor has become more expensive. For example, Chinese wages are rising between 15 and 20 percent a year. According to an August 2011 analysis by the Boston Consulting Group, the higher labor costs in China, the higher productivity of American workers, the transportation costs between China and the United States, and the attendant supply-chain risks will, by 2015, have all but eliminated the difference between what it costs to manufacture goods (at least those that aren't extraordinarily high-volume and labor-intensive) in China and export them to the United States and what it costs to manufacture them here. If you add the reduced linguistic and cultural barriers, the strength of our intellectual property laws, and the opportunities to benefit from the world's leading research universities, you can see why Ford, Caterpillar, and Master Lock, among others, are bringing jobs back to the United States from Mexico, and China. This trend won't mean that American companies will close their current facilities in China; the Chinese facilities can be used to produce goods consumed in a burgeoning Chinese market.

Moreover, our states and municipalities are offering foreign industry attractive incentives to establish facilities in America. Thirty-one states, ports, and municipalities have offices in China seeking investment. One Chinese company, AmericanYunchang, for example, just bought 6.5 acres of land in Spartanburg, South Carolina, for $350,000; in China, a similar plot of land costs four times as much. In South Carolina, electrical costs are four cents per kilowatt; in China it's fourteen cents.[14] Wanxiang, an auto-parts company that has its U.S. headquarters in Chicago, is another Chinese company in America that is succeeding. In 1996, it began acquiring U.S. factories that were in liquidation or bankruptcy with capital it had earned or borrowed in America. As of this writing, it has acquired companies that now employ five thousand six hundred American workers at twenty-eight factory sites. By the estimate of Pin Ni, the president of Wanxiang America, eight hundred of the total number of jobs are new jobs created by growth. The rest are "saved jobs," which could have disappeared without the Wanxiang investment. One in every three American cars produced here use parts made in the United States by Wanxiang. The company has $2 billion in revenue and continues to grow.

According to the U.S. Bureau of Economic Analysis, Chinese annual direct investment in the United States has increased 400 percent since 2008, to $5.9 billion in 2010, which more than doubled the amount invested in 2009. The Rhodium Group, which tracks Chinese investment in the United States, reports that the cumulative total of Chinese-owned U.S. assets is $16 billion—still minuscule compared with the $2.3 trillion value of total existing foreign direct investment in the United States in 2008—the bulk of it from eight countries.[15] In 2010 the United States had the largest inflow of foreign direct investment of any economy in the world.[16]

Whereas technology was once responsible for displacing American jobs, our companies are now coming up with productivity-enhancing new products and processes each year, such as 3-D printing, an efficient way to create all sorts of useful objects by layering material onto design forms, thus eliminating waste and tooling costs. You no longer need a factory in a cheap-labor country or even a contract manufacturer. You just "print" everything, from airplane wings to buildings to blood vessels. Suzanne Berger, chairwoman of MIT's panel on the future of manufacturing, told the *New York Times*: "All of the great new American companies of the past few decades have focused on research and development and product definition—Apple, Qualcomm, Cisco." She pointed out that in those companies the industrial work could be done offshore. "Now," Berger went on, "I think we're at a really different moment. We're seeing a wave of new technologies, in energy, biotechnology, batteries, where there has to be a closer integration between research, development, design, product definition, and production."[17] More manufacturing investment brings with it a whole ecosystem of economic activity; for example, 64 percent of the scientists and engineers in the United States are employed by manufacturers and 70 percent of our research and development takes place in manufacturing.[18] American manufacturing is on the rise. That is good news for America's middle class.

Lifetime Education

To take advantage of our new competitive strengths, we need to increase the number of our modernized vocational schools. For decades, our young people have been told that a four-year college is the only sure route to a good job—and indeed, college graduates do earn more than high school graduates. Currently, only about 50 percent of U.S. high school graduates complete college. That leaves half of our young people with little or no skill development after high school. The sons and daughters of steelworkers and autoworkers know the dignity of blue-collar work. They learned it from their parents. Now it's time for us, too, to reclaim our respect for them. They will be increasingly important to our national future. These are the individuals who, with a little training, would be able to staff the coming manufacturing renaissance.

Recently, the National Association of Manufacturers (NAM) established a program together with America's community colleges to train half a million skilled workers and connect them with a job in five years.[19] The government needs to partner with the private sector to upgrade workers' skills at America's one thousand sixty seven community colleges in far greater numbers than envisioned by the NAM. When a company expands or situates a plant in an area, there ought to be immediate coordination with the local community colleges. For example, Siemens is working with community colleges in North Carolina to train workers for its new high-tech turbine factory that will employ nearly eighteen hundred people. Seimens pays workers who go to school and also supports the community colleges directly.

In addition to providing the skill upgrades, each college should have a significant childcare program so that we don't lose talented single parents who had children when they were too young. America should be a country of second chances. If your fate is cast by age twenty-five, you will lose the upward mobility that is your birthright. We have to deal with the world we have, not the world we wish was ours. Forty percent of children in America are born to a single mother, which means that young women, even if they graduate from high school, end up with a triple burden: they need to care for their children, and they need to work for a living, and they need to get an education in order to get a job that enables them to better support their children. Low-skill factory jobs are dying. On-the-job training is no longer enough, because in fine precision manufacturing, the cost of mistakes in training is prohibitive. Only wise government policy that subsidizes vocational education and childcare attached to community colleges will maximize the skills of our future workforce.

The high-tech sector in America is a wonder. The combination of great scientific universities, vibrant capital markets, and iconoclastic geniuses has brought us constant innovation. The Internet, the digital revolution, social networking, genetic engineering, nanotechnology, ultrashort pulse lasers, artificial intelligence, data mining, robotics—each emerging technology has had disruptive potential. No one knows now what they will bring, but you can be sure they will create a different world for our children, even as they create new jobs in new fields. If there's a deep federal commitment to basic R&D across the board, we'll see a public/private partnership that will serve America well.

Schools are essential if we are to take maximum advantage of the high tech revolution. They should be flexible enough to allow genius to find its own level and workmanlike enough to provide graduates with the basic skills that will prepare them for the jobs that genius will create. The people most responsible for developing those talents are teachers. There are 3,193,830 elementary, middle, and secondary school teachers in the United States. The economic future of the 312 million people in America depends on this 1 percent. Imagine 312 million Americans as a giant buffalo herd and America's teachers as a platform that covers an abyss. The only way the buffaloes can be sure they won't fall into the abyss is if the platform is strong enough. We need to build the strongest possible educational platform to get our citizens from where we are now to the best possible jobs in the future. Investment in the platform, including higher teacher salaries and greater accountability, should be among our highest priorities.

In a world of rapid change a premium will be placed on adaptability. Those who thrive on change will succeed, which means our educational system must not teach to rote tests alone, but in addition to inculcating the basics, must develop students' abilities to adapt, listen and contribute to change—by, say, encouraging them to start a tutoring service or a new company or a new Website that serves their classmates, or a hundred other projects that give them a chance to learn how to innovate in collaboration with others. The first skill needed is empathy—the ability to see yourself in a context of other human beings and figure out how to help them with a task. Those who have learned how to innovate as teenagers will be ready as young adults to take on the changes that will be a staple of the future.

High-tech innovation and an educational system to support it are critical components of our long-term job strategy. But there has to be more. That's where high-quality jobs come in—professional jobs such as engineering, research and development, finance and software production. When international trade expands, these areas grow disproportionately. For example, the U.S. trade surplus in business services has nearly tripled since 2003.[20] Sophisticated data analysis and effective use of information technology will generate even more jobs. Coming down in the wage scale to quality service jobs but generating opportunity for further employment growth are jobs that meet real human needs: long-term healthcare for the elderly that is life-affirming instead of end-of-life warehousing will require trained workers; childcare that allows parents to work and children to flourish needs to be skilled; continuing education and travel and self-discovery all need specialized guides. High quality service jobs such as these, besides providing new jobs opportunities, will produce a more humane country.

Freeing Up Business

Beyond effecting deficit reduction, establishing a giant infrastructure program, making investment in basic research, and subsidizing community colleges, government should reduce the costs it imposes on businesses. Cutting the top corporate tax rate would be one way, but it would have an uneven impact, given the great variation that companies pay because of loopholes. The two most effective actions relate to healthcare and employment taxes. The United States is unique in the way it seeks to provide health care for its citizens. It burdens companies with the responsibility and gives them tax incentives to offset only some of the costs. A company's chief social obligation should be to create jobs; providing for people's healthcare and education ought to be the government's responsibility. If the cost of healthcare could be borne by the federal government with something like a Medicare-for-all program, companies would have more money to pay higher wages to their workers. By eliminating the private insurer, you could save between $350 billion and $400 billion a year in administrative costs.[21] If everyone was covered by the health care system, costs would be easier to control, and incentives could prompt health care providers to compete on price and quality. It could be a win for everyone.

   To raise our standard of living and create more jobs, we also need a dramatic shift in our tax system. The 22 million Americans who are counted as unemployed or underemployed hide the total number of people not working. The Bureau of Labor Statistics reported in 2009 that among the non-institutionalized adult population of 235 million, only about 140 million had jobs, which means that roughly

95 million people were not working. Bringing some of these people into the workforce would be a tremendous benefit, not only for them but for the whole economy. The answer isn't a temporary cut in Social Security taxes. These cuts, done in the name of stimulus, have reduced unemployment very little, even as they have drained money from the Social Security Trust Fund.

Today, 40 percent of federal revenues come from taxes on employment.[22] Every job comes with a 15.3 percent tax in the form of Social Security, and Medicare. The employer pays half and the employee pays half. The employer alone pays the unemployment tax of as much as 2 percent. These taxes act as a tremendous disincentive for companies to hire workers, and mean that the employee has less take-home pay. Try explaining to a young person why the FICA deductions will be good for him in fifty years, and you will see a face full of incredulity. We know the price signal works, so if we want more jobs, we should cut the taxes on job creation. You do that not by cutting the top income tax rate on the "wealthy job creators" but by eliminating the taxes directly related to employment, which affect all companies and all workers.

To replace the funding for these bedrock social programs, for which there is broad public support, we should enact a tax on "things." "Change the relative price of people versus things," says Ashoka founder Bill Drayton.[23] It could be a value-added tax on everything but labor, or a gasoline-tax increase, or a set of taxes on specific pollutants, such as lead or nitrous oxide, or an energy inefficiency tax on, say, the 25 percent least efficient cars, appliances, and commercial buildings. The new taxes would be dedicated to a fund for Social Security, Medicare, and unemployment compensation.[24]

For forty years, taxes on non-labor things or natural resources have been low. Drayton's Get America Working! estimates that the combination of cutting taxes on jobs and increasing them on non-labor factors of production would result in a 30-percent price shift in favor of job creation. More elderly would return to the workforce (68 percent say they want to work[25]), as jobs proliferated. Dependency would drop. In addition, the price shift, according to Drayton, would be so great that it could "increase employment over a capital cycle by roughly 40 million full-time equivalent, new, permanent, sustainable, chiefly good jobs." As more jobs were created, there would be faster economic growth, thereby generating further revenues for government investment.

The groups that will benefit from this tax shift are, first of all, the Americans who have been hit hardest by the recession or have been caught in the structural changes in our economy over the last thirty years. And then there are all those groups who don't count in the narrow unemployment statistics, especially the elderly, the young, people with disabilities, minority dropouts, and women at home or temporarily out of the workforce. They, too, would benefit as the broad effect of the tax shift took hold.

We are so far out of shape as a nation that what's needed is no less than a revolution in our behavior and an overhauling of our patriotism. Galloping personal credit and runaway government deficits can no longer enthrall us. We can no longer entertain the belief that people are basically selfish and markets have all the answers. We need to see our connections, both to one another and between the actions we need to take and the results we desire.

America is like a championship team that has hit a slump. A few losses in a row can make team members begin to doubt themselves. Then something happens to remind them of who they are, what they have achieved, and what they can achieve again. Their ability to overcome adversity is one of the reasons they're a championship team. Never underestimate the resilience of the American people. If you've lost your job and your health insurance and your pension has been cut in half, you dig down deeper and work harder. You refuse to give up. You find some reason to believe in tomorrow. That's who we are. We can lose our homes, our jobs, even our friends or family members, and—like the Joads at the end of John Ford's film of Steinbeck's *The Grapes of Wrath*—we'll go on. "We're the people that live," says Ma Joad. "Can't nobody wipe us out. Can't nobody lick us. We'll go on forever, Pa. We're the people."

7

Government Is
Not the Problem

On a gray March morning in 1933, President-elect Franklin
Delano Roosevelt, wearing striped pants, cutaway, and silk hat,
moved by car up Pennsylvania Avenue to the U.S. Capitol. The
braces on Roosevelt's polio-stricken legs clanked against the sides
of his open car as he got out. Leaning on the arm of his eldest son,
James, he slowly made his way through the rotunda and down the
steps to the Capitol's east front. Preceded onto the platform by out-
going President Herbert Hoover, white-bearded Chief Justice Charles
Evans Hughes, and Vice President John Nance Garner, Roosevelt
was about to be sworn in as president of the United States.

The country was in deep economic depression. Five thousand
banks had failed, and with them went the savings accounts of 9
million Americans.[1] Fifteen million people were looking for work.[2]
There were no jobs. Each failed job search reduced the applicant's

self-esteem and increased his hopelessness. Apartments were repossessed and homes were foreclosed on. Couples moved in with their relatives. Having children or getting a divorce became too expensive. Men sold Christmas cards for a little cash, borrowed off their insurance policies, and stoically stood in bread lines. When the Soviet Union advertised for six thousand skilled workers, offering them jobs in Russia, more than a hundred thousand responded. As literary critic Edmund Wilson wrote from Chicago, "There is not a garbage dump in the city that is not diligently haunted by the hungry."[3]

Confronting the biggest national crisis since the Civil War, Roosevelt stood and, braced on James's arm, approached the rostrum. Veteran broadcaster Ed Hill noted that if Roosevelt had sufficiently overcome his invalidism by forcing himself to walk, he had the personal qualities necessary to lead a nation crippled by economic depression.[4] With a stone-faced Herbert Hoover looking on, the Chief Justice administered the oath of office. Roosevelt's left hand lay on the family Bible, opened to 1 Corinthians ("Though I have all faith . . . and have not charity, it profiteth me nothing"), his right hand extended toward the heavens. He had asked that the oath be administered a sentence at a time, so that he might slowly and firmly repeat the words of the Chief Justice. When they finished, President Roosevelt turned to the rostrum, his face grim and unsmiling, surveyed the crowd of over a hundred thousand as the sun broke through the clouds, and launched into his first inaugural address:

> This is preeminently the time to speak the truth, the whole truth, frankly and boldly. Nor need we shrink from honestly facing conditions in our country today. This great nation will endure as it has endured, will revive and will prosper. So, first of all, let me assert my firm belief that the only thing we

have to fear is fear itself—nameless, unreasoning, unjustified terror which paralyzes needed efforts to convert retreat into advance. . . .

What Roosevelt did here was address the emotional state of the country. He became the symbol of hope; and then he turned to the specific circumstances of the country.

> A host of unemployed citizens face the grim problem of existence, and an equally great number toil with little return. . . . And yet our distress comes from no failure of substance. We are stricken by no plague of locusts. . . . Practices of the unscrupulous money changers stand indicted in the court of public opinion, rejected by the hearts and minds of men. . . . They know only the rules of a generation of self-seekers. They have no vision, and when there is no vision the people perish. Yes, the money changers have fled from their high seats in the temple of our civilization. We may now restore that temple to the ancient truths. The measure of that restoration lies in the extent to which we apply social values more noble than mere monetary profit. Happiness lies not in the mere possession of money; it lies in the joy of achievement, in the thrill of creative effort. . . . These dark days will be worth all they cost us if they teach us that our true destiny is not to be ministered unto but to minister to ourselves and to our fellow man. . . .

In these words, he identified the cause of the peoples' pain. It was not the people themselves, but Wall Street, whose values represented only a sliver of human possibility. He then went on to make specific policy recommendations.

Our greatest primary task is to put people to work. . . .
[T]here must be strict supervision of all banking and credits
and investments. There must be an end to speculation with
other peoples' money. And there must be a provision for an
adequate but sound currency. . . . I favor, as a practical policy,
the putting of first things first.

He had respect for our system of government with its balance
between the legislative and executive branches, and thus he urged
Congress to act on his substantive program or develop one of its
own. And he also put Congress on notice:

But in the event that Congress shall fail to take one of these
two courses, in the event that the national emergency is still
critical . . . I shall ask the Congress for the one remaining
instrument to meet the crisis—broad executive power to
wage a war against the emergency, as great as the power that
would be given to me if we were in fact invaded by a foreign
foe. . . . We do not distrust the future of essential democracy.
The people of the United States have not failed. . . . [T]hey
have made me the present instrument of their wishes. In the
spirit of the gift, I take it.

After the inauguration, FDR went back to the White House,
reviewed the inaugural parade with General Douglas MacArthur,
and then, while a White House reception was in progress, went to
the Lincoln Study, where he presided over the swearing-in of his
entire cabinet, whose members had all been confirmed by the Senate just a few hours earlier.

The next hundred days saw feverish executive and legislative
activity, including proclamation of a bank holiday; federal super-

vision of investment securities; abandonment of the gold standard; the Glass–Steagall Act, which created federal deposit insurance and separated commercial banking from investment banks; establishment of the Civilian Conservation Corps and the Tennessee Valley Authority; drastic economies in government ("Too often in recent history," he told Congress six days after his inauguration, "liberal governments have been wrecked on rocks of loose fiscal policy"); the Agricultural Adjustment Act, which increased farmers' buying power; a program for refinancing mortgages; and direct government employment through the National Industrial Recovery Act.

But it wasn't these measures alone that Roosevelt gave the nation. After a decade characterized by excess and the blind pursuit of self-interest, he reasserted the moral standard that we are each our brother's keeper. He reminded us that the heritage of Americans was not only freedom but a government that would inspire us to—in Abraham Lincoln's words—"Do together what we cannot do as well for ourselves." He was invoking a bipartisan tradition that recognized that there was, along with the sphere of private life and a private economy, an equally important public sphere, in which each of us assumed obligations to all of us.

We hear so often these days about government being the problem. "Would you rather spend your own money or have the government spend it for you?" is the knee-jerk question. If we just got rid of government, some politicians say, our economy would roar back to life. The exact opposite is true. Our history tells us that government action frequently lays the foundation for economic growth. In our current economic circumstances, as I've argued, government is critical to a solution.

Lincoln was the first progressive. He understood that individual freedom was not the only foundation on which America was built. Our government was set up in part "to promote the general welfare,"

as the Preamble to the Constitution puts it. Lincoln proposed the
Homestead Act, which gave public land to individuals who would
settle on it. He granted public land and financing under the Pacific
Railway Act for the construction of a transcontinental railroad, and
he championed education by establishing land-grant colleges across
the country. He knew that lone individuals could not get a college
education if there were no colleges. He knew that the West would
not be fully developed if there were no railroads. It took a government acting on behalf of all the citizens to accomplish those kinds of
things. And in turn, this promotion of the general welfare benefited
individuals. Throughout our history, the development of national
infrastructure—and that includes education as well as highways and
railroads—has enriched individuals. But when a government promotes individual wealth at the expense of the general welfare, the
rich get richer and very little reaches the rest of us.

Lincoln's successor in the wise use of government to promote
the general welfare was another Republican, Theodore Roosevelt,
who was horrified by the concentration of power and wealth in the
hands of financiers and industrialists at the end of the nineteenth
century. Like Lincoln, he saw government as the tool of our collective dreams. He broke up the Trusts, passed pure food and drug
laws, and secured millions of acres for national parks. Woodrow
Wilson, a Democrat, didn't agree with Roosevelt on specifics but
shared the principle of using public power to set the rules of commerce, give average people a chance to better their condition, and
make public investments for the benefit of all. Both of these presidents recognized that the public sphere was essential for the private
sphere to prosper and for its fruits to be shared by the greatest number of Americans. They were presidents for all the people. They
felt a moral responsibility for the nation's welfare and believed that
citizens working together could make our democracy the envy of

the world. Their ethos was simple: Care about your fellow citizens, not just about yourself, your family, your friends, but also about your country and even those strangers in your midst whom you may never know.

When General Dwight Eisenhower, a Republican, became president in 1953, he continued in the footsteps of Lincoln, Teddy Roosevelt, Wilson, and FDR by establishing the Interstate Highway System, passing the National Defense Education Act, and accepting the New Deal as a permanent part of America. As the former commander of U.S. forces in Europe during World War II, he had an appreciation not only for the industrial might of America's private sector, which had helped us win the war, but also for the spirit of Americans on the field of battle who had risked their lives both for their comrades and for all of us, because they believed that America's form of government was worth dying for. He understood that individuals acting alone could not build a society or win a war; public institutions had to have the power to act on behalf of the citizenry against the invincible forces—hurricanes, drought, wildfires, pandemics, market crashes—that threaten us all. His vice president, Richard Nixon, would continue in the liberal Republican tradition that government should not be dismantled but used to make America stronger. Far from attempting to repeal Social Security or Medicare, President Nixon worked with a Democratic Congress to advance the public's interest. His proposals for catastrophic health insurance, affirmative action, and welfare reform, while less generous than the Democratic alternatives, amounted to a broad governmental commitment to the lives of ordinary Americans. Explaining to ABC's Howard K. Smith, in early 1971, his plan to propose a budget that would wind up in the red, he declared, "I am now a Keynesian in economics," by which he meant that government could and should help stabilize our economy.[5]

The bipartisan consensus that government exists in part to promote the general welfare was demonstrated in 1964 when Democrat Lyndon Johnson won 61 percent of the vote against Republican Senator Barry Goldwater. The scale of the defeat did not deter Goldwater's true believers, who had vanquished the liberal Republican Nelson Rockefeller in the primaries and wanted, among other things, to repeal Social Security and end the TVA. They only redoubled their efforts to capture the government, repeating consistently the same sullen refrain: "The government is the problem. . . . The government is the problem. . . . " When Ronald Reagan declared, in his 1981 inaugural address, that "government is not the solution," it was the antithesis of FDR's inaugural address forty-eight years earlier. Although his vice-presidential selection of George H. W. Bush was a bone tossed to the pragmatic wing of the party, Reagan's electoral success brought to Washington many ideological Republicans who did not believe in the legacy of Lincoln, the Roosevelts, or even Eisenhower. They emphasized pursuit of self-interest as a way to secure the general interest. Under their narrow definition of common responsibilities, any government investment in the health, education, or welfare of individual Americans was seen as government trampling on individual liberties. Taxes were a form of robbery, and transfer payments, such as Social Security or Medicare, were a form of highway robbery. Nature was there to exploit. Government programs were paternalistic. If you were poor or unemployed or both, it was undoubtedly your own fault, and government should do nothing to help you. They preached a self-centered view of individual responsibility.

Reagan followed this agenda by cutting taxes, which the ideologues thought would create pressure for defunding government programs. But Reagan did not throw out the other constitutional purpose—"to provide for the common defense." The combination of tax cuts and sizable increases in defense spending resulted in a whopping budget deficit. Although the political tone of the administration was ideological, Reagan himself seemed pragmatic, and the people around him, such as Chief of Staff (later Treasury Secretary) James Baker, wanted to govern more than they wanted to dismantle the New Deal or turn the clock back on the welfare state.

As it turned out, Reagan did not shut down government; there was more stability than revolution during those years. Reagan accepted catastrophic health insurance for the elderly. When his 1981 tax cut proved a fiscal nightmare, he agreed to the largest tax increase in our peacetime history. While his actions to promote the common good have largely been forgotten by the general public, his anti-government rhetoric has not, and he is repeatedly invoked as a Tea Party icon. But the real Reagan would flunk the "no new taxes" litmus test required of today's Republican candidates.

When George H. W. Bush was elected, the pragmatic Republicans were back in charge. While his administration might not have been a second Eisenhower administration, as some liberal Republicans had hoped, it was an administration of reasonable people who were willing to compromise in order to get something done. Our next president, Bill Clinton, a brilliant, gifted politician, had been shaped by the Reagan years, when the ruling rhetoric was about government being the problem. During those years, he had been an active member of the Democratic Leadership Council, a group whose purpose was to develop centrist policies that would allow Democrats to win in an age of anti-government sentiment. He passed a significant deficit reduction package in his first year, but when Republicans won control of Congress in 1994, instead of asserting the moral principles of the Democratic Party holding that the American enterprise was at its best when we took responsibility not only for ourselves and our families but also for our neighbors, our country, and the planet, Clinton decided it was better to appropriate so-called Republican issues such as crime and welfare, move to the center, and appeal to the electorate with less-than-ambitious symbolic proposals couched in phrases from focus groups. Maybe that path was his only political chance, but he went too far when, in his 1996 State of the Union address, he said, "The era of big government is over," and commentators agreed that he sounded just like Reagan. Clinton was re-elected, but the unwanted side effect was the muffling of the Democrats' moral vision, while conservative Republicans kept hammering away against Big Government in the moral language of right and wrong.

When George W. Bush won in 2000, the Republican communication juggernaut had already provided him with the new vocabulary. Freedom from government, the primacy of the individual, financial success as the ideal—these were the values that had been repeated over and over by the Republican machine, permeating the media, for nearly forty years. All Bush had to do was mouth the words and then, after he won, turn the government over to the ideologues. He did both. There were no Jim Bakers in the Bush II White House. For every Karen Hughes and Condoleezza Rice, there were ten Karl Roves with grand designs for dismantling the government, embodied most starkly by the attempt to "privatize" Social Security. Science was out, ideology was in. Global warming was not a problem. Evolution and creationism were equally valid academic subjects. Stem-cell research was immoral. A helping hand was the business of church charities rather than government. Still, even George Bush evinced some bipartisanship in foreign and domestic policy. His war in Afghanistan had support in both parties. His education bill, No Child Left Behind, had Democrats Ted Kennedy and George Miller as partners. His bill to include a drug benefit in Medicare was a significant expansion of government, even as it rewarded pharmaceutical companies by denying Medicare the right to negotiate lower drug prices for recipients.

Today we're in a different world. Virtually no Republican can adopt the positions of past Republican presidents and survive the political firestorm from the Tea Party. The right-wing orthodoxy of the Tea Party is unforgiving, uncompromising, and relentless. It is a radicalism that has always resided in the Republican Party but formerly characterized only a fraction of its members. Now it's the prevailing view. Indeed, the congressional Republicans are more nihilistic than Reaganesque. They seem to want only to obstruct.

For those who argue that only the private sector is important, I'd say, "Look around." Without government, there's no economic prosperity. There are measures that benefit everyone: airports, airline safety, roads, bridges, schools, sewers, dams, mass transit, power grids, ports, water systems, food safety, weather forecasts, law enforcement, disease monitoring, drug safety—and many more. These are public goods. Without them, the private sector would wither. Moreover, a kind of selflessness obtains among people in government. I'm not talking here about elected officials—presidents, senators, representatives, governors—but the dedicated employees who run city water systems or make sure the subways run or oversee the dams that provide us with electricity and irrigation. The very best professional expertise informs the government's judgments on environmental quality and food, drug, and airline safety. We are able to trust in the integrity of those decisions, because they are being made for all of us—and, indeed, most government employees assiduously attempt to serve the public welfare.

As in any organization, government has its share of incompetents and superfluous employees, and their unions often seem to be more interested in job security than in a job well done. But when presidents disparage civil servants, as Ronald Reagan once did, they disparage all of us. Thousands of extraordinary individuals serve in the FBI, the SEC, the CIA, the State Department, the Food and

Drug Administration, and the National Oceanic and Atmospheric Administration, among others, who could be making a multiple of what they earn in their government jobs if they were in the private sector. If a business that has witnessed their competence lures them away with a higher-paying job, the government team loses another good player to the private sector, which is already bursting with talent. Altruistic public employees often find themselves having to choose between their public service and their family's economic welfare. If too many of them move on, and too few talented young people make the decision to serve, this disparity in competence between the public and private will grow, power will concentrate in even fewer hands, and all of us will suffer.

Many of our great historical American achievements—among them the Lewis and Clark expedition, the Interstate Highway System, the Tennessee Valley Authority, the reclamation of our arid West, the oversight of our public lands, the mapping of America's mineral wealth, the breakthroughs at the National Institutes of Health, the effectiveness of our law enforcement, and the honest collection of our taxes—are examples of government workers acting on our behalf. But the present financial crisis and its destructive ramifications—depressed housing prices, stagnant wages, high unemployment—have been brought to us by people who want *no* government involvement in our lives and by those Democrats who collaborated with them in breaking down the basic government safeguards that FDR set in place during the Great Depression, the repeal of Glass–Steagall being the signal example. The irony is that, as linguistics professor George Lakoff of the University of California at Berkeley has pointed out, government controls very little of our daily lives.[6] In the United States, it is the private sector that determines which doctors we can see, what food we eat, the news that gets to us, the loans for our homes. The private sector, with its dynamism and innovation, plays a necessary role in our society—but not a sufficient one. You need a way to "do together what we cannot do as well for ourselves," and only government is large enough to meet that need.

We need one another now more than ever before. The wealthy have to see, as many do, that their luxury is irrelevant in a world where schools don't work, roads and bridges deteriorate, and more and more people lose faith in the American dream. Yet simply raising taxes on the wealthy (which should be done) will not solve our problems; government, too, needs to be accountable for results in its management of the public trust. Those who believe that government can do great things must ensure that it functions effectively. People need to have confidence that their tax dollars are not being wasted. In an attempt to micromanage government, Congress burdens it with so many narrow reporting requirements from so many committees that fulfilling them leaves little time left to do the important work of running the operations of government. At the same time, the Congress does very little effective oversight of how a particular program measures up against its broadly stated goals. Instead of passing a new budget, Congress simply extends the previous budget for a few months, weeks or days. "Just kick the can down the road" too often becomes the mantra.

Government reorganization is not always reform. It is often an excuse for not doing reform. There should be more government mediation and fewer government lawsuits. Allowing the bureaucracy greater flexibility in means and greater responsibility for results is essential. Otherwise government employees become simply box-checkers trying to cover their behinds and keep their jobs while the problems remain unsolved. Such behavior will not accomplish the necessary things that only government can do for all of us.

Sometimes the bureaucratic rules are in conflict or incomplete. For example, the budget might allow for new computers from approved vendors but not for new software that will allow the computers to perform as they are intended to. No one sees the whole picture. Instead, government agencies have little communication with one another. (Think of the FBI and the CIA right before 9/11.) The reform of governmental information systems is critical to a more effective government. Yet the daunting costs of doing so are further complicated by arcane purchasing rules that create interminable delays and often prompt vendors to enlist the help of members of the club. A cold mountain stream needs to roll through the federal bureaucracy and the halls of Congress so that government can be revitalized for the twenty-first century.

Can we all do better?

8

A Model for All
Other Governments

The United States, from its inception, has been ambivalent about its role in the world. Protected behind two oceans since the mid-nineteenth century, and continental in size, it has long enjoyed an inherent security. Europe, Africa, and Asia have suffered wars on their own territory. For the United States since the mid-nineteenth century, war was, in the words of the popular World War I song, always "over there."

History

From our nation's beginning, as Arthur M. Schlesinger emphasized in the examples below from his *The Cycles of American History*, there was a question about how much we should involve ourselves in the affairs of other nations. Thomas Jefferson, in his first inaugural address, warned his countrymen against "entangling alliances." John Quincy Adams, in his July 4 address to the House of Representatives in 1821, went further than Jefferson. He said of America,

> Wherever the standard of freedom and independence has been or shall be unfurled, there will her heart, her benedictions, and her prayers be. But she goes not abroad, in search of monsters to destroy. She is the well-wisher to the freedom and independence of all. She is the champion and vindicator only of her own. She will commend the general cause by the countenance of her voice, and the benignant sympathy of her example. She well knows that by once enlisting under other banners than her own, were they even the banners of foreign independence, she would involve herself beyond the power of extrication, in all the wars of interest and intrigue, of individual avarice, envy, and ambition, which assume the colors and usurp the standard of freedom. The fundamental maxims of her policy would insensibly change from liberty to force. . . . She might become the dictatress of the world. She would be no longer the ruler of her own spirit.

In 1847, the venerable statesman Albert Gallatin wrote, in a pamphlet entitled *Peace with Mexico*, that America's mission was "to be a model for all other governments and for all other less-favored nations; to adhere to the most elevated principles of political morality; to apply all your faculties to the gradual improvement of your own institutions and social state; and by your example to exert a moral influence most beneficial to mankind at large."

Henry Clay, in a debate on a Senate resolution condemning Austria for its suppression of the 1848 revolution in Hungary, argued that the resolution made judgments about foreign nations:

as their conduct may be found to correspond with our notion and judgment of what is right and proper in the administration of human affairs [and assumes] the right of interference in the internal affairs of foreign nations. . . . But where is to be the limit? . . . Where, again I ask, are we to stop? Why should we not interfere in behalf of suffering Ireland? Why not interfere in behalf of suffering humanity wherever we may find it?

Clay warned against opening "a new field of collision, terminating perhaps in war, and exposing ourselves to the reaction of foreign Powers, who, when they see us assuming to judge of their conduct, will undertake in their turn to judge of our conduct." Some twenty years later, President Ulysses S. Grant, soon after assuming office, noted that although America identified "with all people struggling for liberty . . . it is due to our honor that we should abstain from enforcing our views upon unwilling nations and from taking an interested part, without invitation, in the quarrels . . . between governments and their subjects."

For much of the nineteenth century, America concentrated on building our own nation—settling the West, dealing with the conflict over slavery, developing our natural resources, growing our economy, perfecting our system of government. There were brief, violent nationalistic episodes, such as the wars against Mexico, Spain, and the Philippines, but by and large we stayed out of foreign conflicts. We were not lured into the intrigues of Europe, and we successfully blocked other nations from intervening in the affairs of our hemisphere.

Nevertheless, a conflicting belief intensified in the early twentieth century: namely, that American foreign policy should be rooted in ideals, not national interest alone. Immigrants who had fled their home countries for America had begun urging the United States government to take action against those countries. Didn't the Declaration of Independence express universal values such as human rights? Shouldn't we champion those human rights everywhere? Ethnic lobbies brought the horrors taking place in the old country to the attention of their congressmen and demanded action. The sense that America was special in the world and had a unique mission had been a part of our hearts from the beginning; now that feeling morphed into condemning other countries for the way they governed their people and calling on the United States to change their behavior. These exigent pleas prompted Teddy Roosevelt, the Rough Rider and no stranger to the use of military power, to warn Congress in 1904 that we should be careful about using force abroad:

> Ordinarily it is very much wiser and more useful for us to concern ourselves with striving for our own moral and material betterment here at home than to concern ourselves with trying to better the condition of things in other nations. We have plenty of sins of our own to war against, and under ordinary circumstances we can do more for the general uplifting of humanity by striving with heart and soul to put a stop to civic corruption, to brutal lawlessness and violent race prejudices here at home than by passing resolutions about wrongdoing elsewhere.

For congressmen intent on pleasing their constituents, you could have your cake and eat it too. You could advocate U.S. involvement—on behalf of the Irish, the Armenians in Turkey, the Jews in Russia, Eastern Europe, and the Near East—and know that the president was not about to involve the United States in those distant places. No sons of your immigrant constituents would die for the home country.

Passing a resolution was easy. Doing something about a particular atrocity was more problematic. Ought we to apply our standards to all other countries? To a few? Were human rights to be defended only in service of the national interest, or was the pursuit of human rights an absolute guide to foreign policy?

Woodrow Wilson's worldview was colored by his Christian morality. As a skilled student of government and an admirer of the British parliamentary system, Wilson believed to his very core in the virtue and "sacred mystery" of democracy. When he became president in 1913, he had had very little experience in foreign policy. After a campaign that was almost exclusively about domestic policy, he remarked that it would be ironic if his administration were to be consumed by events outside the United States. Yet, he was possessed of a kind of democratic messianism, determined that America would relate to the world as a moral force.

China had created a more representative government in 1912 after the fall of the emperor, and Wilson made sure that the United States was the first major power to recognize it. Soon afterward, China degenerated into despotism. When President Francisco Madero of Mexico was assassinated by troops loyal to the usurper Victoriano Huerta, Wilson recalled the U.S. ambassador, froze Mexican government funds in the United States, and, after a short wait, used American military power to depose the dictator Huerta in favor of the constitutionalist Venustiano Carranza. Not long afterward, Carranza turned virulently anti-American, and when Wilson sent General John J. Pershing and his troops into Mexico in pursuit of Pancho Villa, a Mexican revolutionary who had shot up the U.S. border town of Columbus, New Mexico, he guaranteed Mexican hostility for several generations.

Wilson looked at European politics with disdain, deeming it selfish power politics at its worst. During the early years of World War I, he maintained U.S. neutrality and ran for re-election in 1916 as the man who "kept us out of war." As the war dragged on, Wilson used diplomacy in an attempt to get the belligerents to the table. He wanted a negotiated settlement and proposed a lasting peace that recognized the rights of small nations and guaranteed freedom of the seas and self-determination for subjugated peoples. The Germans rejected his proposal. Wilson was shocked. On April 2, 1917, he went before Congress and asked for a declaration of war against Germany, announcing, "The world must be made safe for democracy."

As the war proceeded, Wilson's rhetoric intensified. In a sweeping statement, he said that the war aimed to bring "destruction of every arbitrary power anywhere that can . . . disturb the peace of the world." Otherwise, "Everything that America has lived for and loved and grown great to vindicate . . . will have fallen in utter ruin. . . . Force, force to the utmost, force without stint or limit, the righteous and triumphant force shall make right the law of the world and cast every selfish dominion down in the dust."[1]

Two million American troops turned the tide for the Allies, and the Germans finally sued for peace. The nation was jubilant. At Versailles, Wilson's ambitions were enormous. He wanted to change the structure of international relations so that the power politics that had, from his perspective, led to the war would forever be subsumed under the functioning of a kind of world government embodied in a League of Nations. Wilson's counterparts from Britain, France, and Italy had different ideas. They were interested in reaping the spoils of victory and ensuring with draconian measures that Germany would never again be able to go to war. Wilson's dream of the League floundered, as had his earlier policies in China and Mexico. When the United States' participation in the League of Nations was voted down in the Senate, Wilson left office a sick and dispirited man. He had raised the hopes of millions with his rhetoric of democracy. The League's eventual failure raised the question of whether his ideas had been workable or advisable. Senator Henry

Cabot Lodge, for one, had persisted in asking how the League's purposes would be enforced.

Still, Wilson left a legacy of democratic messianism that would shape the statecraft of future generations. Franklin Roosevelt's "Four Freedoms" address in 1941, the United Nations charter in 1945, and the U.N.'s Universal Declaration of Human Rights in 1948 all took their inspiration from his efforts. Determined to prevent history from repeating itself, and more and more beguiled by the idea of democratic exceptionalism, the United States, as World War II came to an end, led in the creation of the United Nations, the World Bank, the International Monetary Fund, and the General Agreement on Tariffs and Trade.

Beyond the aspiration, there were big questions left unanswered. Were all countries—no matter how large or how central to the strategic interests of the United States—to be treated the same? Who would assume the cost in money and lives to bring this dream to reality? By what criteria would we decide whether or not to intervene on behalf of human rights?

George Kennan, the diplomat who authored containment policy against the Soviet Union, raised a more fundamental point in discussing the Versailles peace treaty: "[It] was the sort of peace that you got when you allowed war hysteria and impractical idealism to lie down together in your mind . . . when you indulged yourself in the colossal conceit of thinking that you could suddenly make international life over into what you believed to be your own image."[2] President Dwight Eisenhower seems to have agreed with Kennan. Acting from the older tradition of national interest, he ended the war in Korea, resisted involvement in Vietnam, and refused to intervene in the Hungarian uprising against the Soviet Union.

The country welcomed President John Kennedy, who, in his campaign for the presidency, had moved to the right of Richard Nixon on defense, claiming, among other things, that Eisenhower had allowed a "missile gap" to develop with the Soviet Union. In his inaugural address, he asserted that "we shall pay any price, bear any burden, meet any hardship, support any friend, oppose any foe, in order to assure the survival and the success of liberty." Kennedy conveyed a new energy, epitomized by the Peace Corps—an energy that touched people both here and abroad, who seemed captivated by the idea that the most powerful man in the world could be so young and so dashing. Reality soon destroyed their illusions about youthful magic. Kennedy, reflecting inexperience, approved the Cuban émigrés' disastrous invasion at the Bay of Pigs. Less than a year and a half later, in a remarkable testimony to personal growth, he prevented nuclear war by giving the USSR an acceptable way out of the Cuban missile crisis. But the country continued to see every potential conflict through a Cold-War lens. Slowly but inexorably, Kennedy was led into the quagmire of Vietnam, and his successor, Lyndon Johnson, only deepened our involvement, unable to distinguish an honorable withdrawal from defeat.

The United States had been attempting to control events in other countries since the end of the Korean War: In 1953, there was the CIA-sponsored coup against Prime Minister Mohammad Mosaddegh, the elected leader of Iran, followed by the elevation of the despotic shah. The coup against President Jacobo Árbenz Guzmán of Guatemala in 1954, the Bay of Pigs invasion, and the coup against Chile's democratically elected Salvador Allende in 1973 reflected our belief that interference in the politics of other countries was our prerogative. In the post–Vietnam era, this kind of intervention continued, with efforts to depose dictatorial or communist regimes in Angola, Nicaragua, El Salvador, and Panama—efforts that offended millions of Americans in spite of arguments invoking the ideals of the Founders or our principled opposition to communism.

The moralism in foreign policy that diplomat George Kennan so decried in his lectures on foreign policy at the University of Chicago in 1950 was once again fashionable by the end of the 1970s. Wood-row Wilson's democratic messianism was back in vogue. President Jimmy Carter espoused a muscular human-rights policy but was wise enough to use only economic and diplomatic means to enforce it, even as he authorized covertly aiding the Mujahideen in Afghanistan in their war against the USSR. President Ronald Reagan committed U.S. troops to Lebanon and Grenada while sponsoring covert wars in Central America. The first Iraq war, in 1990–1991, revived the argument about "just wars" and the United States invoked the U.N. charter's prohibition on members invading another member nation as justification for our involvement. President George H. W. Bush conducted the war flawlessly and ended it by keeping the promise he made to his allies: that Iraq would be evicted from Kuwait, not occupied, and Kuwait's sovereignty would be restored. After the dissolution of the Soviet Union, President Bill Clinton used the just-war argument to justify our intervention in Serbia in defense of human rights, while not responding to genocide in Rwanda—raising the old question posed to democratic interventionists: "Where do you draw the line?"

With each of these exercises of military power, America became more self-righteous. We invaded on principle, which seemed to make violence acceptable—and besides we were omnipotent, so no one could stop us. There was no countervailing force to our entry into or instigation of wars intended to rid the world of this or that tyrant and "make the world safe for democracy." Most of these interventions were brief and accomplished with allies—Who wouldn't want to curry favor with the world's only superpower?—which further convinced us that the world was swinging our way. Our democratic example could now be spread more aggressively. We decided to expand NATO eastward, even though the organization's purpose—to counter Soviet military power—had evaporated with the dissolution of the USSR and the end of Russian communism. What could Russia do about it? Democracy was on the march—and Russia was invited to come along.

When we bombed Serbia in 1999 and the Russians protested, our response, in effect, was that we had a right to intervene because in the sectarian violence between Serbs and Albanian Kosovars, we had concluded that the Serbs were more in the wrong. In 2008, we recognized the independence of Kosovo from Serbia. For the first time since the Helsinki Accords of 1975, a territory had been taken from a nation against its expressed desires. President George W. Bush was received in Albania by cheering crowds, just like Wilson in Paris in 1919. In 2010, the Council of Europe issued a report pointing out that Kosovo's prime minister, Hashim Thaçi, in the last decade, headed a group once responsible for heroin trafficking and trade in human organs. Yet again, self-determination had created something quite different from what democratic interventionists had envisioned.

Then 9/11 happened, in the first year of a new president who had campaigned against nation-building abroad. Ten years, two wars, and more than $1 trillion later, during the administration of Bush's successor, Barack Obama, we finally killed the leader of the 9/11 strike, Osama bin Laden. By that time, our rhetoric had gotten us into a no-win situation.

We maintained that we were in Afghanistan not for revenge but to remake a society in our image. We were there so Afghanis could rule themselves freely, women could receive equal treatment, and the standard of living could rise. Slowly it became clear that the reality of Afghanistan and Iraq was quite different from the liberal democratic ideal promoted by proponents of the invasions. We never really knew who our friends were in the government circles or among the intelligence sources in either country. We took our NATO allies into the Afghani conflict in part to show the reach of NATO's new, broader, self-justifying mission. Instead, we may have generated, along with the NATO bombing of Libya, forces of disillusionment and discord that may well lead to NATO's demise. As in the fog of war that obtained in Vietnam, our only recourse was to stay longer and send more troops. We had trouble recognizing that our version of democracy might not neatly apply in deeply divided tribal cultures.

For those of us who believe that our example is our strongest asset in world affairs, what example do these wars convey to the world? How have they furthered our long-term interests? What have they said not only to the Muslim world but also to China, India, Brazil? What have they said to the billions of young people around the world who are looking for leadership they can admire and trust? What did we think we were doing by using military power to force democracy on countries that didn't ask for it, at great expense to our own citizens in terms of money and lost lives? In the end, we have just been talking to ourselves, trapped in assumptions and rhetoric from another time. There has to be another path.

I would go back to George Kennan and re-read his opposition to messianism in our foreign policy. While Americans feel that democracy—our democracy—is the best form of government ever invented, they are divided about whether we should fight wars to impose it on other countries. That's called imperialism, and it requires occupation for decades and trillions of dollars to finance. There is no shortcut. And we have never aspired to be the English or the Ottomans or the Romans. The prosecution of the wars in Iraq and Afghanistan contradicted the values that inform our view of ourselves. Bombing citizens of another country is now called "collateral damage." We seem to think that a quick apology and restatement of our anti-terrorist purpose is sufficient to cleanse our hands. Yet such self-justification only further erodes our example. Who, after all, would want to emulate a country whose only contact with you is the humming of a drone?

A country needs a strong enough military to defend itself from genuine threats. The use of that military, however, should be rare. The lesson of the Cold War was that deterrence requires not military action but only the development of a credible threat. In the 1990s, though, a new question arose: "Why have a military if we don't use it?" My response is that militarizing too many disputes undermines our example and our claim to leadership and inevitably, given the law of unintended consequences, leaves us in no-win situations. The results of military actions are unpredictable. Thinking of military intervention as a handy policy tool you can pull out when the time is right ignores the messiness of war and underestimates its potentially negative effects on our political objectives, not to mention the cost in lives and treasure.

Lead by Example

So, what is the example we should be setting—the stance from which we should seek to lead the world? I think it should be the example of a pluralistic democracy with a growing economy that takes everyone to higher ground. By "pluralistic" I mean a tolerant, multiracial, multiethnic country in which people seek to learn from one another's uniqueness but also accept what it means to be an American: our language, institutions, and the political ideals that hold us together. By "democracy" I mean a country in which people not only vote but also participate in the affairs of their communities, and a country whose judicial system renders judgments based on the law, our present circumstances, and our hoped-for future, not on politics, ideology, your ability to pay lawyers, or a too-narrow construction of the Constitution. By "a growing economy that takes everyone to higher ground," I mean a country in which upward mobility is possible and bad luck at birth doesn't ensure bad luck for a lifetime; a country that encourages and rewards innovation and gives all Americans the educational tools they need to excel; a country that ensures its citizens' access to health care; a country in which, if you work hard, you can have a good retirement. I believe this example has wide appeal. It is not fully realized. Still, if people around the world see that we're on the path to its fulfillment, they will be with us. And we should invite them to join us.

In the twenty-first century, the intelligence of people will determine the future. Our free society can be the magnet for some of the world's brightest minds if we deliberately, carefully, and intelligently open ourselves up. Lee Kuan Yew, the former Prime Minister of Singapore, has said that while China has a talent pool of 1.3 billion people, the United States, given its history of accepting the foreign born, can draw talent from all 7 billion people in the world.[3] We should welcome the arrival of doctors, scientists, writers, mathematicians, computer specialists, language teachers, and other such talented professionals from abroad. The United States has always benefited from immigration of talented people. One of the side effects of the persecution of the Jews that preceded the horror of the Holocaust was the immigration of Jews who have immeasurably enriched American society. As a meritocracy, we should welcome those who can get admitted to our universities or provide us with needed skills in government agencies, science laboratories, hospitals, and elsewhere. For example, we need an intensive effort to train Americans to effectively teach science and math, but in the interim the only way we can educate our kids in these critical areas is with the help of foreign teachers. The former mayor of Chicago, Richard M. Daley, once told me he was trying to import math and science teachers from China and Eastern Europe to the Chicago school system because he couldn't find competent Americans. Any time a foreign student gets an advanced degree from an American university, he or she should automatically get a green card. We should also be open to those with entrepreneurial spirit who have the resources and want to start a business. Finally we should welcome not just the brightest or those with resources but also, as we always have done, those in limited numbers who just want a better life and show the ambition to seek it here. Surely, in a land as large as ours, we can make room for the energy, drive, and optimism that immigrants bring to our shores.

Ever since the Great Depression, the economic prospect that has most terrified policymakers has been a labor surplus—unemployment. Even now, when unemployment remains at an unacceptably high level, it's difficult to imagine that within fifteen years we will have a labor scarcity. The magic number needed to maintain a stable population is 2.1 children per woman. In 2010 we were at 1.93. Forty-seven of the most advanced countries are at 1.6 or less.[4] As baby boomers retire over the next decade, we will need new workers to make the economy grow, pay the Social Security and Medicare taxes necessary to fulfill our promises to the elderly, and produce the goods that they will demand. We either increase our birth rate, or accept more immigrants, or settle for slower economic growth. Look at Japan or Russia, which are both losing population because of low birth rates and hardly any immigration. They are committing slow-motion national suicide. Would you rather have hardworking and sometimes brilliant foreigners paying into our Social Security system and making retirement more comfortable for elderly Americans, even as they create jobs for working Americans, or a smaller U.S. working population that will be unable to sustain the program at its current level in a few years? We need more young people to carry the load for the increasingly larger number of retirees. Demographics don't lie.

On occasion, conflict has accompanied large waves of immigration to America. It happened when the Irish and the Germans came in the nineteenth century and the Italians and Eastern Europeans in the late nineteenth and early twentieth centuries, and it happens now with Mexicans and Muslims. Since passage of the Immigration and Nationality Act in 1965, which abolished the national-origins quota system, the face of immigration has changed; there are fewer Europeans and more Central Americans, Asians, and Africans. We have absorbed these immigrants into our larger culture with a minimum of negative repercussions. When I heard a recent radio interview with Linda Sarsour, an Arab American woman preparing to run for the New York City Council from a Brooklyn district that is heavily Moroccan, Algerian, and Palestinian, I was moved by her obvious devotion to the sense of possibility that is the birthright of all Americans. Newcomers have always added value to America. Look at New York or Jersey City or San Jose or Houston or Miami or Chicago in the last thirty years; each has been revitalized by immigrant communities that have come to America to build lives they couldn't lead in their homelands. A Silicon Valley entrepreneur I know, a Pakistani Muslim married to a Hindu woman from India, once remarked to me, "Where else in the world but America could we be happy and accepted?"

Japan forbade non-Japanese to enter its island nation until the 1850s, and it still has very little immigration, even in the face of a declining birth rate. China has treated its minorities as groups to be controlled, not as individuals with valuable potential. Europe has historically focused on differences among its member states more than on commonalities. France, Germany, the Netherlands, Norway, and Britain have little history of genuine assimilation. As these societies age and birth rates drop, their economic future is bleak without immigration. Yet when immigrants do come, they trigger a more negative cultural and emotional reaction from a larger segment of the population than does immigration in the United States. At its extreme, the xenophobia produces riots in Britain and France and the murder of innocent children on an island in Norway by a right-wing fanatic who thinks immigration and assimilation are ruining Europe.

In contrast, our history shows that each wave of immigrants added definition to what it meant to be an American. America is not static but constantly changing. Having overcome the deep racism of its history and integrated successive waves of immigrants, the United States, more than any other country, should welcome the pluralism that is growing in the age of the Internet and whose successful management could inspire admiration around the world.

With regard to Mexico, our neighbor to the south, the answer is not building walls to separate us. Walls can be circumvented—witness the flourishing drug trade that still plagues us. For those who want to stop the border crossings, the answer is promoting economic growth in Mexico through trade and establishing a farsighted guest-worker program here. Who would leave their families, live in miserable conditions, and subject themselves to arrest if they weren't ambitious and didn't believe in a better future? Immigrants from Mexico and many other countries come to America for a job, often willing to work hard at things many Americans simply don't want to do. Doctors end up driving taxis, accountants clean houses, and when you call a plumber to fix your leaking pipe, an electrician to rewire your house, a mason to build a stone wall, someone to work in your restaurant kitchen or mow your lawn or care for your child or sit with your elderly parent, inevitably, in many places in America, you will get an immigrant. Until our culture makes blue-collar work once again noble, many Americans won't want to do it. Increasingly, the only people who will know how to deal with the nuts and bolts of our society will be people who learned their skills in another country.

The path to U.S. citizenship should be open to anyone, but it should be a definitive choice. Until the late 1960s, people who became U.S. citizens weren't allowed to vote in their home country's elections. The naturalization oath still includes a renunciation of allegiance to any other country. Yet today it is possible to carry an American passport and the passport of another country. So you have a foot in two places. With that American passport, if things go to hell in the place you come from, you can always flee to America with no questions asked. America is your fallback. You can have dual allegiance. In the past, American immigrants wanted to become Americans. Their future was here. They had a profound reason to participate in the affairs of their country, volunteer for its army, teach their kids English, learn our history. Now for some U.S. passport holders America has become a place of convenience, not commitment.

China

Our future will depend more on economic competition than on military conflict, and China is our number-one challenge. The United States continues to regard China as if it were just like any other country. It isn't. Its population and its culture make it a formidable economic competitor—but not a military adversary. While armed conflict with its neighbors has played a role in Chinese history, China has not launched a war of aggression far beyond its periphery since the Manchu expeditions in the eighteenth century. It ended its overseas expansion and opted out of maritime imperialism. Instead, it exercised its power economically by granting access to the Middle Kingdom. Today, the Chinese have modernized this technique. Companies and leaders censor what they do and say about China out of fear of government retaliation against their interests there. The more deeply companies become entwined with the Chinese economy, the greater China's leverage.

China's defense budget is growing, true, but ours is still larger than the defense budgets of China, Russia, Germany, England, Brazil, and India combined.[5] Given how many times foreign powers have invaded China over the centuries, it is understandable that the Chinese want a defense capability that will allow them to defend their country against all comers, but they're smart enough not to waste their treasure in military adventures. Just look at Taiwan. China claims that it is a province of China, but it has taken the long view that in time the natural evolution of economic connections and cultural affinity will bring Taiwan back into the Chinese fold. Preparing for a military competition with China is old-think. Economics is the challenge of the twenty-first century. The Chinese have internalized this fact; we seem to have forgotten it. As Bill Overholt, senior research fellow at Harvard's Kennedy School has said, "After World War II, we stimulated the economic growth of our allies in Europe, Japan, and Southeast Asia and we won the Cold War through the economic revival and dynamism of Western Europe, Japan and friendly Southeast Asia. The Soviet Union lost through economic failure. Our military was vital to *protecting* the core nation building strategy, but the core strategy was economic and institution building."[6] Militarizing every disagreement in the world as an act of first resort not only will bankrupt us but also misses the nature of the threat we face and further erodes our example.

The Chinese are strategic thinkers above all else. They're able to decide on a long-term policy and follow it. For thirty years, the Chinese have said that their first priority was developing their own country, not seeking military conquest of their neighbors. They want to move people out of poverty. They want to raise the country's living standard. They want to amass wealth. In order to do that, given their 1.3 billion people and limited natural resources, they need to influence events outside China without resorting to military aggression.

Just a few examples of how China's strategic thinking translates into action: They intend to build three high-speed rail lines to the west. The first line will go southwest from China to Singapore. The next will go through Central Asia to Turkey and then to London (a modern version of the ancient silk route), and the last will go across Russia to Moscow and on to Berlin. These projects will cost billions of dollars and take decades to complete. When finished, they will also give China access to the natural resources of Central Asia, Siberia, and Southeast Asia.[7] Meanwhile, in the United States, we can't even finish the rail line from Dulles International airport to downtown Washington, DC.

Another example of China's long view is its aim to dominate its neighbors through the management of water resources. China needs electricity, and hydropower is one of the best renewable energy sources. The Chinese government intends to build several giant dam projects in addition to the one at Three Gorges. The strategic implications arise because they will build the dams on rivers that flow into India and Southeast Asia. By controlling the headwaters of the Brahmaputra, Irrawaddy, and Mekong, they will have leverage over countries whose economic welfare depends on those rivers. So, from within their own country and in a way that improves their own economy, they are establishing themselves as the regional hegemon.

Yet another example of farsightedness is what China is planning in the vicinity of the United States: They trade more than ever with Brazil and Venezuela, and they have suggested to Colombia that they help finance the construction of a rail line between the country's Pacific and Caribbean coasts. Such a route will be an alternate to the Panama Canal, which itself is being widened to accept larger container ships. We have known about this widening of the Panama Canal for a decade, but Norfolk, Virginia, is still the only Atlantic port in the United States large enough to accept the new container ships that will transit it. Meanwhile, China has acted. Li Ka-shing, the wealthiest man in Hong Kong, has built a giant port in the Bahamas that can accept the new ships. The port will offload cargo for transport to American ports that can accommodate only the smaller container ships. The Chinese building of ports doesn't stop in North America. They have built a port in Gwadar, Pakistan, which has given them their first listening post on the Indian Ocean, close to the oil routes of the Persian Gulf. In addition, they are building or upgrading ports for governments in Burma, Bangladesh, and Sri Lanka.

China is even active in the North Atlantic. Last summer, Huang Nubo, one of the richest Chinese real-estate tycoons, offered to buy three hundred square kilometers of Iceland. When he was asked why he needed such a vast tract of land, he said that he wanted to build a resort. Iceland, a non–EU sovereign country between Europe and America, will have a much larger role to play in a world where the warming of the planet will make hundreds of thousands of its acres usable. It will also be a transit point in Asian-Atlantic trade using a new polar shipping route. The Icelandic government said no to the investment.

The Chinese are locking up resources—oil, minerals, agriculture— all over the world, from Africa to South America to Australia. They even showed up in my small hometown on the Mississippi in search of iron ore and a port from which they could export the smelted pellets. You can gauge the magnitude of their effort by looking at Western Australia. There's such a shortage of labor for the region's iron, coal, and gold mines that companies pay heavy-machinery operators as much as $220,000 per year.[8] Every morning at 4:45 a.m. at the Perth airport, hundreds of workers appear at a labor exchange and offer their services to the highest bidder. Planeloads of workers dressed in yellow mine uniforms disembark after two weeks in the mines and another group of similarly clad miners boards the planes for the next two-week shift.[9] Chinese demand has created the boom.

A final example of China's strategic thinking relates to its long- term economic aspirations. China has long been a cheap labor country, but in 2007, the 17th Congress of the Communist Party affirmed its intent to develop the nation's high-tech sector. China has often required foreign companies in some industries that locate in China to take a Chinese partner. It has ratcheted up the pressure on the high-tech companies to transfer technology to these joint ventures. Reverse engineering and other forms of appropriation then allow wholly owned Chinese companies to compete with those foreign companies on international markets. According to the German Engineering Federation, nearly two thirds of German machine-building companies suffer piracy of products and trademarks, resulting in €6.4 billion in lost revenues, with China being responsible for 80 percent of those losses.[10]

Everything China learns from their foreign partners moves them up the value chain to higher-paying jobs. With more than 6 million college graduates a year (up from 1 million a decade ago), China needs higher-paying jobs, so it is building advanced industries such as aviation, high-speed rail, sophisticated telecommunications, and oceanographic and space exploration. It allocated $19 billion in a multiyear grant for nanotechnology in its 2009 stimulus package (total U.S. spending on nanotechnology by government, venture capital, and the private sector is $6 billion). In 2011, China became the world's largest energy user and has tripled its patent filings in the last five years, growing a remarkable 56 percent in 2010 alone. It even offers gold-plated salaries to star foreign researchers to come and work in China. The aim is to steadily produce world-class economic players across industries and globally. Sany, a Chinese machinery group that produces everything from mobile cranes to excavators, has grown 50 percent per year ever since its founding seventeen years ago, with revenues in 2009 of $4.5 billion. After years of partnership with German companies in China, Sany in 2010 launched a production facility in Germany, competing in terms of price and quality with one of Germany's cherished industries on its own turf. In 2012, global

German machinery sales dropped 23 percent, to €178 billion, while the Chinese machinery industry sales rose 12 percent, to €300 billion. Germany is no longer number one in machinery.[11]

While China has been busy enhancing its national power for generations to come, the United States has been engaged in two wealth-sapping wars. We have poured our treasure into the desert sands. The predominant press and policy attention of the last decade has been focused on the Middle East. While we have endless debates about promoting democracy, getting reluctant countries to the negotiating table, winning hearts and minds, defining and re-defining what is a strategic interest, the Chinese have been laying the groundwork for economic dominance in the twenty-first century, and they are doing it without firing a shot. A Chinese official once asked me, "Why are you Americans so interested in all those small countries?"

The front page of the *New York Times* on October 29, 2011 had two stories side-by-side that illustrated our relative positions in the world. The headline on the China story read, "China Is Asked for Investment In Euro Rescue." It described European government officials imploring the Chinese to buy bonds in the new euro bailout fund. The Chinese predicated any investment on strong conditions, such as getting Europe's support for recognizing China as a market economy in the World Trade Organization—which would essentially make it harder to level trade sanctions against China. The story confirmed that China is using its strong export trade economy, vast currency reserves, and large market to play a global power game. Right next to this story was a headline that read, "Western Companies See Prospects for Business in Libya." While China increasingly calls the shots in a new global economy, we pick over the bones of our latest military adventure in the Middle East.

On September 4, 1989, Deng Xiaoping offered seven guidelines culled from China's history to direct its future: "Observe calmly, secure our own position, cope with affairs calmly, hide our capacities and bide our time, be good at maintaining a low profile, never claim leadership, and seize the opportunity to make a difference."[12] China is methodically following Deng's strategy, to secure its advantage in sector after sector, country after country.

The challenge in Chinese martial arts is to change movements continuously in order to overcome an opponent with skill, rather than brute force. The I Ching tells a leader to be modest and rule by example rather than by fear or diktat. The Chinese seem to have applied these approaches in their relations with the world. We don't have a clue how to play their game. They're all about subtle strategy that leads to dominance. We're all about tactics that lead to destruction. We see our defense in terms of global power projection. They see theirs in terms of cyberpower and other assymetric security strategies that can disable the war-fighting capabilities of any would-be invader. Our approach is very expensive; theirs is much cheaper. While we're busy defeating ourselves by our braggadocio, impatience, and desire to lead like a general on a white horse parading before the applauding crowd, the Chinese ruling elite engage in a three-year, comprehensive debate about the role that China wants to play in the world. While 40 million Americans watch *American Idol,* 100 million Chinese are watching a twelve-part series of hour-long TV programs on *The Rise and Fall of Nations.*

China's game plan is there in its history—all we have to do is read it. The ancient Chinese Empire sought to enrich others so it could enrich itself more. The goal is incompatible with traditional notions of war. We invade Afghanistan, and the Chinese buy up one of the world's great mining tracts there. We fight the Taliban to create democracy, but the Indians build the Afghani Parliament building. We wage a war in Iraq to kill a dictator and bring freedom to the Iraqis, and the oil companies of other nations get large oil concessions. When President Obama puts troops in Australia, the Chinese shrug; they know that they can get the mineral resources of Australia for China (which is all they really want) with economic power, because Australia finds such deals are in its interests too. The Chinese don't do press releases; they just steadily advance their position.

The real irony is that if we understood how to play the game, we could enhance the power of our own country. What is required to secure our future is skill at paradoxical thinking—that is, China simultaneously can be our greatest ally in creating a better world and our most formidable rival. As F. Scott Fitzgerald wrote, "The test of a first-rate intelligence is the ability to hold two opposed ideas in the mind at the same time and still retain the ability to function." Instead of racketing around the world like some stereotype of a warrior king, we need to find the quiet center of our ideals and lead from there. We need to make change our friend and the development of our own country our number-one objective. In such a world, as the possibility of Chinese purchases of $1.2 trillion in U.S. infrastructure bonds illustrates, there is no reason that the United States and China could not be the best of partners, even cooperating to ameliorate global problems, such as climate change or poverty.

The pressure we should bring on China is for them to follow international norms on intellectual property and state subsidies, to say nothing of the rule of law. China is in transition from a relationship-based society, which is inherently corrupt and inefficient, to a society based on rules that in China's future will be necessary to deal with everything from governance of foreign investment to structuring of a national healthcare system to management of scarce resources. The current endemic lawlessness and official corruption were caught by a friend of mine who recently wrote from Beijing, "A country where people can't trust what they eat, the trains they ride, or the products they buy, can't secure a stable future." Chinese leaders are acutely aware of those problems and confront them daily. They also often protest international rules such as the accounting and governance requirements of the New York Stock Exchange or the maritime treaties of the 1860s, but when they agree to join a part of the international system, we have to hold them accountable for abiding by the rules of that system. If we believe they have violated provisions of the WTO, we should use the organization's dispute-settlement mechanism to make our case. That's what it means to have an international system that works. Disagreements will be inevitable. Resolving them with a minimum of chest-thumping will serve all parties.

When certain Chinese officials claim that the South China Sea is a core interest of China's, along with Tibet and Taiwan, some Americans conclude that the comment represents national policy. It is as though every Congressman's utterance were to be taken as national policy. In fact, a phalanx of Chinese generals, diplomats, and academics has said that it is not national policy.[13] China is prepared to negotiate its territorial claims in the South China Sea; the only question relates to whether the negotiation will be multilateral or bilateral. Their claims to Tibet and Taiwan are non-negotiable. The real danger zone in Asia is the East China Sea, the body of water that separates China from its longtime Asian rival Japan. A miscalculation there by either side could lead to a military conflict fueled by intense nationalism in both countries.

As for espionage, we should be realistic, not emotional. Blocking Chinese espionage is not war, any more than is our spying on them. The intelligence craft has been a part of international life from time immemorial. When someone waxes indignant about it, I recall the classic line in Casablanca: "I am shocked—shocked—to find that gambling is going on in here!" Yet Chinese espionage has taken on a new form and risen to a new level. We need to be aware of the nature and breadth of hacking efforts coming out of China and take appropriate countermeasures. Our companies, particularly in the high-tech area, are under persistent, withering attack. Many of them have called on the government for help. Economic security and national security are no longer separate domains. As the secretary of defense's 2010 annual report to Congress states somewhat breathlessly, "The heavy use of outsourcing of computer and consumer electronic production to China, not only by American but also Japanese, Taiwanese, German and South Korean firms has helped create a Chinese cyber threat that now compromises the security of the Western world." Joel Brenner writes about the nature of cyber war in his book, *America the Vulnerable: Inside the New Threat Matrix of Digital Espionage, Crime and Warfare*, noting that "the objective in warfare would not be killing or occupying territory, but rather paralyzing the enemy's military and financial computer networks and its telecommunications. How? By taking out the enemy's power system. Control, not bloodshed, would be the goal. . . . "[14] It is unlikely that this possibility will ever become reality with China, but it is better to be prepared than caught by surprise. Money spent on cyberdefense would be money well spent.

In addition, we have to understand the effects of our own actions on China. U.S. ships and airplanes mounting intelligence-gathering operations in international waters at least twelve miles from China's coast fall under the accepted category of espionage. Using that intelligence to execute simulated attacks on Chinese targets in order to assess Chinese defenses and responses in a potential military situation amounts to more than espionage and is needlessly provocative. Imagine how the Congress would react if it learned that the Chinese were just twelve miles off the coast of California running simulated attacks on our mainland. We have to ask ourselves whether the military information we get about a country with which there are no imminent hostilities is worth the political cost. These events, which are known to Chinese authorities, along with the wide television coverage in China given to United States-Japanese-South Korean live ammunition joint naval exercises, send the message to the Chinese people that America sees China as the enemy. If this impression hardens, there inevitably will be a Chinese reaction.[15] Is that any way to build a common future? It is to be hoped that those on both sides of the U.S.-China relationship will find cooperation more advisable than conflict. To miss the win/win potential of our relatioship would be a tragedy.

Adjusting to the reality of Chinese economic power may prove difficult, given our current assumptions about how to operate in the world. For example, when the Palestinians applied for admission to UNESCO, the education and cultural arm of the United Nations, a law passed in another era required a cutoff of U.S. support for UNESCO. The premise of the law was that thanks to our economic clout (we supply more than a fifth of UNESCO's budget), we could prevent UNESCO from admitting the Palestinians. The threat failed and the Palestinians took their place in the organization. In a world with growing Chinese power, such action, like a clumsy martial arts move, could backfire. China could simply fill the void anytime we backed out, enhancing its soft power and making us look like the spoiled child who picks up his marbles and goes home when he doesn't get his way. The time has come for us to wake up and start playing the geopolitical game of the twenty-first century, not the one of the last half of the twentieth.

The Future

None of this means that America should become isolationist. We have genuine economic interests in the world. There are also people who want to kill us. But anti-terrorism should be as much a political strategy as a military challenge. You can't influence the Muslim world primarily with military action. You need to be consistent in your ideals, steadfast in your commitments, strategic in your approach. You need to understand the history of Muslim societies and the depth of the demographic, economic, and educational challenges

they face. You have to determine how best to encourage the influ-
ences of moderate Islam in various countries. You have to acknowledge the role of Islam in the lives of more than a billion and a half
people and seek to find common ground on a spiritual level, which
will help us on the political level. You have to invest in such a strategy for the long term, with the knowledge that it might take a decade
to show results. Sometimes, objectives clash. The policy we follow
to ensure our access to oil might be different from one for dealing
with al-Qaeda. Clarity about our central objectives will facilitate our
decision-making.

   We need a strong defense against the real security threats of the
twenty-first century—cyberwar and bioterrorism as well as nuclear
proliferation—and against the unforeseen: developments in ethnic
strife; alliance shifts; technological breakthroughs; and availability
of natural resources such as water, oil, and arable land. We won't
have the wherewithal to counter those real threats if we perpetuate
the old military structures of the Cold War or seek to right every
wrong in the world. The most important geopolitical fact, and one
central to the reach of our economy, is that since 1945, the United
States has controlled the seas. We can monitor, stop or sink any
ocean-going vessel whether it is carrying oil, food or nuclear components. In a world increasingly dependent on trade, such capacity
is critical to our power. To secure our military position, we must
keep a modernized global navy, along with the associated space systems. And we need to create adaptable land forces—speed and
flexibility will determine the winner in many future conflicts—able
to rapidly convert vast quantities of information into action and
equipped with hypersonic weapons, the drones of today on steroids.
The defense budget should be used to counter the threats we face,
not (as Eisenhower might have observed) to produce a jobs program in congressional districts across America or (as George Ken-

nan might have observed) to remake other cultures and spread the gospel of democracy around the globe.

Our democracy is blessed in many ways. One of them is that we have a dedicated and loyal military and a skilled intelligence community. Each has an important role in national security, but they are directed by our political objectives, which are set by our president and the foreign policy team he chooses. The real judgment and leadership come in setting those objectives. If you ask the generals responsible for fighting the war in Afghanistan for their opinion on whether we should leave, their answer would almost always be no—an answer you want from can-do, patriotic soldiers. Tell them to run through a wall, and they will try. Tell the generals that you have decided, from your perspective as president, that the war is not in our interests and seek their counsel on how to get out. They will salute and say, "Yes, sir." That is the difference between policymaking and combat readiness. To protect our country we need both, but in our democracy the policymaker is rightly primary.

In the 1990s, after the end of the Soviet Union, many in Washington had a unipolar moment. We were the single omnipotent superpower. If you read history, you knew that such an idea rested on pure hubris. As if the arrogance weren't bad enough, we then acted militarily on the belief in our omnipotence, and in so doing endangered our long-term interests. If we don't change our views, we will fall further and further behind in our ability to deliver on the promises our leaders have made to promote a pluralistic democracy that takes everyone to higher economic ground. Our nation will become a tarnished example and weaker in the eyes of the world. The choice is ours.

We can all do better.

9

Empowering the People

There have been times in American history when our democracy sputtered, failing to address the real issues that faced the nation. Anger rose—occasionally violence exploded—and then there was a democratic adjustment that let our noble experiment in self-government proceed. Frequently the remedy was a broadening of the franchise, thus enlarging the pool of opinion that officeholders had to consider when making decisions.

In our country's early years, the only people who were allowed to vote in America were white men with property. By the 1840s, however, most states had given the vote to all white males (convicted felons excepted). In 1870, the Fifteenth Amendment to the Constitution enfranchised African American males (although poll taxes and intimidation just as quickly disenfranchised most of them), but not until 1920 were women given the vote. Native Americans were allowed to vote, at least in some states, after passage of the Indian

Citizenship Act in 1924, and citizens of the District of Columbia were enfranchised in 1961. Ten years later, the voting age was lowered from twenty-one to eighteen. Each wave of new voters shook up the system, raised new issues, created new pressures for change, prompted new political coalitions. Each broadening of the franchise reduced the number of people outside the system who, with no stake in the country's future, had provided kindling for the demagogue's match.

Another remedy for the problems of our democracy has been to give people a more direct say in it. Although the Founders created an indirect democracy, in which the people elected representatives to speak for them, there was resort to direct democracy when the need arose and it was deemed workable. From the beginning of the Republic, U.S. senators were selected by state legislatures; the thinking of the Founders was that they would represent the states (and do so free of pressures from the populace), whereas the members of the lower house would represent the people and be elected by them directly. The system worked reasonably well until the decade leading up to the Civil War, when state legislatures deadlocked on a regular basis and U.S. Senate vacancies lasted months or more. In Indiana in the 1850s, the conflict between northern Indiana Republicans and southern Indiana Democrats left a Senate seat open for two years.

After the Civil War, the problem persisted; between 1891 and 1905 there were forty-five deadlocks in twenty states, but now the cause was as often corruption as sectional passion. State legislators were controlled by party bosses, industrialists, and financiers. A Senate seat was often bought—if not directly, then by the offer of a sinecure to the new senator in exchange for his fealty to the particular interest: a bank, a railroad, an oil company. Between 1866 and 1906, nine cases of bribery were brought before the Senate. Senator William Stewart of Nevada symbolized the age. Wallace Stegner, the great writer on the American West, has described him:

Robust, aggressive, contentious, narrow, self-made, impatient
of "theorists," irritated by abstract principles, a Nevada
lawyer, miner, Indian-killer; a fixer, a getter-done, an in-
defatigable manipulator around the whiskey and cigars, a
dragon whose cave was the smoke-filled room, Big Bill Stewart was one to delight a caricaturist and depress a patriot. But
he was also, in his way, a man of faith: he believed in Western
"development," and he believed in the right of men—himself
among them—to get rich by this "development."[1]

The negative reaction to congressional corruption was widespread. In the 1890s, the Populist Party, whose members hailed
primarily from the West and Midwest, put direct election of U.S.
senators in its platform, reminding adherents that Andrew Jackson
and his supporters had been early proponents of direct election in
the 1830s. Western progressives awoke to the problem first. In 1907,
Oregon—and soon after, Nebraska—created popular elections for
senator that bound state legislators to select whomever the voters
had selected, and by 1912 twenty-nine more states, including Maine,
New Jersey, and Pennsylvania, had similar provisions. Still there was
opposition to the idea. Proposed constitutional amendments were
defeated every year between 1893 and 1905 by the Republican old
guard in the Senate, the protectors of financiers and industrialists.
Advocates of direct election found an unlikely ally in William Ran-
dolph Hearst, who hired young muckrakers to report on the wrong-
doings of power brokers. A series of articles in Hearst's magazine
Cosmopolitan by David Graham Phillips called "The Treason in the
Senate" accused both Democrats and Republicans of "advancing the
industrial and financial interests of the wealthy classes of the country." The Progressives and the Populists were gaining strength. An
aphorism of the day went, "It is harder for a poor man to get into the
Senate than it is for a rich man to enter the Kingdom of Heaven."

But it wasn't until the advocates of direct election demonstrated they had thirty-six of the forty-eight states—the necessary three quarters—ready to sign up for a constitutional convention to deal with the issue that the opposition collapsed. Congress passed the Seventeenth Amendment establishing direct election of senators in 1912, and it was ratified a year later.

By the mid-twentieth century, the engineers of democratic reform had returned to broadening the franchise. The Voting Rights Act of 1965 ensured that what had been promised to African American men in 1870 and African American women in 1920—the right to vote—was now fully realized. It eliminated the racist tricks that for nearly a century had blocked their attempts to vote in the South. When the poll taxes and literacy tests and blatant intimidation became illegal, black Americans lined up for hours to vote in free elections for the first time. American politics changed for the better.

Dr. Martin Luther King Jr. believed deeply in the ideals of the Founders, and with courage and confidence he moved America forward, first with civil disobedience and then by widening the vote. President Lyndon Johnson never forgot the lives of the poor Mexican American fifth-, sixth-, and seventh-graders he'd taught in south Texas. When he became president, he said, "It never even occurred to me in my fondest dreams that I might have a chance to help the sons and daughters of those students and to help people like them all over the country. But now I do have that chance— and I'll let you in on a secret—I mean to use it."[2] The visionary leader and the genius politician shared a dream of what America could become, and together they forced Congress to deal with issues it had so far all but ignored. Even the stain of racism could be washed away by the river of broader democratic participation. Once black Americans saw that they could effect change through the ballot box, all the romantic 1960s talk about "revolution" dissipated and our democracy was strengthened.

Johnson left office a broken and highly unpopular man. After his heart attack in 1955, his doctors had forbidden him to smoke cigarettes, which he dearly loved, and as president he kicked the habit. Then, on the day Richard Nixon was inaugurated and LBJ boarded Air Force One to fly back to Texas, he lit up a cigarette. He knew there was nothing left to live for. He had squandered his popularity and legendary skills on a war he couldn't win. Nevertheless, he directed that all of his presidential papers be opened to the public, and after his death Lady Bird Johnson granted access to all the audio recordings. The former President and First Lady were willing to entrust his legacy to the fair-mindedness of the American people and let history be his judge. When you listen to the recordings, what emerges is the picture of someone who knew how to get things done. In just the first three years of his presidency, he signed into law nearly two hundred landmark bills. He was a master of compromise. His conversations with Republican Minority Leader Everett Dirksen of Illinois are classics. LBJ appealed to Dirksen's patriotism in their discussions on civil rights and to his judgment on Vietnam. He appealed to Dirksen's political self-interest as well, offering him projects for his state while pleading for one or two Republican votes for a particular bill. What comes through in these recordings is the efficacy of horse-trading for a noble purpose.

The recordings also illustrate the trust Dirksen and LBJ had in each other, a trust built on knowing the other as a human being. You couldn't imagine either one blasting the other in the press or making negative insinuations about the other's character. In a collegial body, there is no substitute for knowing an opponent at a deeper level than the political one. When I was in the Senate, there was genuine personal interaction among Democrats and Republicans—though occasionally your view of a fellow senator hardened. For me, it was difficult to give the benefit of the doubt to Jesse Helms of North Carolina. The gay-bashing and race-baiting in his Senate service and his campaigns turned me off. His opposition to the creation of a national holiday for Martin Luther King was the final straw. I didn't want to talk to him. I thought not only that we had nothing in common but also that he represented a kind of evil that still lingered in the American shadows.

Then one day, out of the blue, I got a call from his wife, whom I had never met. Mrs. Helms told me that their nineteen-year-old granddaughter played basketball in North Carolina and was coming to Washington. Would I be willing to meet her and share some tips about the game? Taken aback, I said, "Sure!" and that if we met at a playground near my house I'd take a look at her shots. Three weeks later, at exactly 6:00 p.m., a beat-up old green Oldsmobile pulled up at the playground. In it were Senator Helms, Mrs. Helms, and their granddaughter. All three got out of the car and proceeded to the blacktop court. We said hello. Senator and Mrs. Helms sat on a bench on the sidelines, and the granddaughter and I took the court. She would shoot, and I'd throw the ball back to her so she could shoot again. I told her to stand and shoot, dribble to her left and shoot, then to her right and shoot. Within about fifteen minutes, I realized she was a very good player indeed; I could tell she loved the game and had spent long hours working at it. Meanwhile, the Helmses sat on the bench smiling and watching their granddaughter swish shot after shot. I showed her some moves, we talked about defense, rebounding, passing. After about an hour, we were finished. Senator and Mrs. Helms got up and thanked me warmly, joined their granddaughter, got back into the Oldsmobile and drove off. From that day on, my view of Jesse Helms was more nuanced and less self-righteous. I could never again see him solely through the lens of his issue positions and related tactics. For me, he would also be a doting grandfather sitting courtside watching his extraordinary granddaughter make shots from all over the court.

In today's Washington, collegiality appears to be dead. Few congresspeople live in the capital. Socializing between members of different parties now occurs infrequently. Members rush back to their district so as to avoid the charge, popularized by former Speaker of the House Newt Gingrich, of being a Washington insider. Anything resembling the Dirksen–LBJ bond seems an impossibility. Pat Moynihan used to have Republicans and Democrats together to his house for dinner. So did I. If you're only in town three nights a week, and each of those nights is a fund-raiser, there's little time for getting to know your colleagues of the opposite party. I often think of Hamilton and Jefferson hammering out the compromise that put the United States on a sound financial footing in 1789. They found a way because they loved the country. Today, too many politicians love their jobs more—and their campaigning never stops. The old four/two rule, whereby you were a senator legislating for four years of your six-year term and a senator campaigning for two, seems so long ago. Its abandonment has resulted in very little progress on the things people care about, like jobs, pensions, education, the environment, deficit reduction, and infrastructure.

Today, as at the end of the nineteenth century, there is a deep and growing animosity toward our government. In addition to the pain of the middle class, the poor believe that politicians are indifferent to their plight. The investor class fears that runaway deficits will ruin the country. The young are skeptical of the whole concept of representative democracy. In times like these, the political extremes attract a wide audience, promoting measures that at best are unlikely to work. The Tea Party and the Occupy movement fit this category. Coupled with ignorance, these movements can produce sentiments that might be funny if they weren't so pathetic: "Keep your government hands off my Medicare," one Tea Partier roared at a town hall meeting in the summer of 2009.[3] If the delegates to the 1787 Constitutional

Convention had been as unwilling to find common ground as today's political class (particularly Republicans), we would never have ended up with a Constitution.

Slowly, the politician has become another species to the average person. This disillusionment with those we elect is ominous, because, in our representative democracy, they're supposed to speak for us. The lack of collegiality is serious because the engine of our democracy from the beginning has been skilled compromise. Today that seems a lost art. We sorely need to create a government that reflects the moderate middle, which is willing to compromise, rather than the ideological extremes. One way to do that is to change the way we draw congressional district lines. Right now, in almost every state, they are drawn every ten years, mostly by partisan legislatures. The result is that out of 435 House seats, only 50 are competitive and only 21 of those are very competitive.[4] The rest are comfortably Democratic or Republican in registration and voting pattern. If I'm running for Congress as a Democrat in a 60–40 Democratic district, I don't have to listen to Republican voters in my district. All I have to worry about is a primary. I do everything I can to avoid being challenged in a primary, which means I pay undue attention to the fringe of my party. Democrats move to the left. Republicans move to the right (witness the influence of the Tea Party). We can take the redistricting decision out of the hands of partisan legislatures and give them to citizen commissions (as has been done in California) or to a panel of federal judges, with the instruction to create districts as compact and competitive as possible. Candidates who have to reach across the aisle in order to get elected will have established a habit that will serve them well when they arrive on Capitol Hill. When politics no longer rewards extremism, extremism will decline. The state of our two major parties is such that a growing number of people are registering as independents. According to Beyond Red vs. Blue: Political Typology, a Pew Research Center Report in May 2011, more people (37 percent) considered themselves independent than identified themselves as Democrats (32 percent) or Republicans (25 percent).

In 1986, in my second Senate term, two huge bills, tax reform and immigration reform, became law. Both won bipartisan support. I was deeply involved in tax reform, which had the support of a Republican president, a Democratic chairman of the House Ways and Means Committee, and a Republican chairman of the Senate Finance Committee and passed by wide majorities. On the immigration bill, I remember going to see Alan Simpson, a Republican senator and its main author. I had a list of twenty-two questions about the bill. He and I sat alone, with no staff present, and he answered all of my questions. At the end of our hour, I told him he had my support. I didn't even know the "Democratic position," if there was one. The bipartisanship that existed in 1986, and in the Social Security compromise three years earlier, seems impossible today.

The rigidity of our politics makes everyone a mouthpiece instead of an independent thinker. Polling says that 82 percent of the American people are worried about jobs. What do Republicans propose to do about this? Their only response is, "Don't tax the rich." Why? Because, according to them, the rich are the primary "job creators." Notice the choice of words: Republicans appear to hope that the phrase will persuade the electorate that Republicans care about providing jobs. A closer analysis of their policy reveals that they don't want the federal government to do anything substantial to relieve unemployment. Most of the "job creators" are not rich but middle-class small-business owners, and most hiring decisions are based on a judgment about their sales, not the marginal tax rate. But the spinners and the pollsters are betting that people won't look at the fine print and the media won't point out the obvious facts

Although the views of conservative Republicans are contrary to the interests of the majority of Americans, many of those Americans vote Republican. Why? I believe one major reason for this paradox is that Republicans use a moral language, whereas Democrats use policy language. In a contest between the heart and the mind—that is, between deep conviction and facts—conviction wins every time. Berkeley linguistics professor Lakoff has observed that swing voters are people who can be conservative on fiscal policy and liberal on social policy (or conservative on foreign policy and liberal on domestic policy), but no matter which side they fall on, they tend to respond to conviction.[5] When one party speaks from moral principles on an issue that swing voters care about—say, conservative fiscal policy—and the other party speaks with the facts about, say, liberal social policy, the moral-language position prevails.

Over the years, Republicans have made a sustained effort to build a national organization resembling a pyramid, with money (lots of it, from very rich people) forming the base, followed by a level for think tanks that generate radical ideas, such as privatizing Social Security. On the next level are pollsters and pundits, who express those ideas in language that achieves the maximum political advantage (i.e., don't tax "job creators"; don't support the "death tax"). At the top of the pyramid is the presidential candidate, who, by the time he has run the gauntlet of the primaries, is locked in the prison of party orthodoxy. Often that orthodoxy fails to reflect the views of a sizable number of Republicans, who feel disinherited by the reactionary fringe controlling their party.

Democrats have a different problem. They have long tended to look for the charismatic leader who, by the force of his or her personality, can single-handedly transform the country. The exemplar is JFK. Democratic candidates in subsequent presidential elections have donned the mantle of youthful, energetic leader. Gary Hart, Bill Clinton, Barack Obama all fit the mold. The problem with such an approach is that in searching for Prince Charming, Democrats have neglected to build their party with ideas from the grass roots up. There is no Democratic pyramid; there are only fan clubs.

Our politics today has boiled down to two competing ethics: the ethic of caring, which implies collective action and is usually associated with Democrats, and the ethic of personal responsibility, which implies individual action and is associated with Republicans. Every campaign debate begins from these poles. But given our present national circumstances, both ethics are necessary. Take pensions: Collective caring would require protecting Social Security, especially since it's the only retirement income for 35 percent of America's elderly. Individual responsibility would require each of us to save if we want more than a subsistence retirement. Yet most Americans don't save enough. The Survey of Consumer Finances has reported that if you're sixty-five, you should have saved $300,000 if you want a comfortable retirement. The current average is $60,000. Forty-six percent of all working Americans have less than $10,000 saved.[6] Take health care: Collective caring would mean that everyone in America should have access to health care; individual responsibility would prompt us to take care of our own health by paying attention to what we eat and drink and how often we exercise. One third of Americans are obese and another third are overweight, according to the Centers for Disease Control and Prevention. The healthier we are, the less we cost the system and the more money is available for insuring all Americans. Take education: The state can provide good schools, but families have to provide a context for maximum achievement and the students have to do the homework. Or, take democracy: Laws can ensure the franchise for all Americans, but individual citizens must exercise their right to vote. Caring and responsibility go only so far separately; together, they build the foundation for America's future. And when they're combined with research, public investment in infrastructure, and a new tax system to make us more competitive in the twenty-first century, you have the recipe for rising living standards and fulfilled dreams.

We can all do better.

The Major Party Duopoly

For whatever historical or ideological or media-driven reasons, the system just isn't working for the majority of Americans. We need a return to the idea that the answer to the problems of democracy is more democracy. That means finding a way for people's voices to be heard so that politicians will listen and politics will once again be a vehicle to make America better for more of our citizens.

Every two years, we elect a House of Representatives and one third of the Senate. Every four years, we select a president. The candidates we choose from have nearly always been nominated by our two major parties. These parties form a duopoly, blocking the emergence of a third party through campaign finance laws and other election regulations. The Federal Election Commission, which rules on a candidate's adherence to the campaign finance laws, is composed only of Republicans and Democrats. No independents. Should a third party begin to get traction because of its message, one or both of the parties will steal its agenda, arguing that only they can make something happen in the Congress because virtually all members of Congress are in one or the other of the parties. It's a circular argument that has worked for a hundred and fifty years.

The last successful third party was the Republican Party, founded in 1854, which fielded Abraham Lincoln for president only six years later. After 1860, the high point of third parties came in 1912, but the circumstances were unique. A popular president, Teddy Roosevelt had decided not to run in 1908, selecting as his successor William Howard Taft; he even left the country so as to give Taft the chance to establish himself free of Teddy's shadow. The portly gentleman from Ohio won the election and subsequently proved to be a great friend of big business. When Roosevelt returned from a two-year around-the-world tour, he was appalled by President Taft's program. After trying unsuccessfully to get Taft to adopt the progressive positions of the previous Republican administration, Roosevelt decided to form his own party, the Bull Moose Party, and ran for president against Taft in 1912. The Democrats' nominee in 1912 was New Jersey Governor Woodrow Wilson. A fourth candidate of substance was the Socialist Eugene V. Debs, a founder of the Industrial Workers of the World. The race was one of the best contests in American history, full of larger-than-life characters, playing on a world stage and debating their differences honestly and eloquently. Wilson took 42 percent of the vote, Roosevelt was second with 27 percent, and Taft got only 23 percent. Debs got 6 percent, a high-water mark for an American Socialist.

After 1912, the only third-party candidates to receive electoral votes were Bob LaFollette in 1924, Strom Thurmond in 1948 and George Wallace in 1968. LaFollette won only his home state of Wisconsin. Running as a Dixiecrat, Thurmond won four states in the South, primarily on a racist appeal; and Wallace, as the candidate of the American Independent Party, won five Southern states. All other prominent third-party candidates—John Anderson in 1980, Ross Perot in 1992, Ralph Nader in 2000—failed to get even one electoral vote. They played big in the media, but they had no chance of winning—which is not to say that they had no effect on our country's trajectory. Bill Clinton won in 1992 because Perot took votes from George H. W. Bush, and George W. Bush won in 2000 because Ralph Nader took votes from Al Gore.

Very rarely, a major party can do something surprising. In 2008, Barack Obama upended the Clinton establishment and stormed to victory. Smart and eloquent, he was also an innovator, using the Internet to organize and fund-raise. He touched a deep chord in America's consciousness, and people responded. Of the $746 million he raised for his campaign, more than half came from donations of less than $1,000 and more than 30 percent came from contributions of $200 or less, often made on several separate occasions. The strategic insight of the Obama team was to realize that if he won all the caucus states by quietly out-organizing Hillary Clinton, he would have to win fewer of the primary states to claim the nomination and would force Clinton to spend much more money as the campaign season wore on.

His communication success came from his having the same story throughout the campaign: "Elect me and together we can change Washington and then do great things again." Clinton had three stories about her identity: experienced professional, inevitable nominee, and Mama Bear defending the middle class. John McCain seemed to have had a new story every week. Obama's victory was unique, related as much to his compelling persona and message of hope as to the country's desire to get beyond its history of racism and the collapse of its international reputation during the Bush administration.

Nevertheless, despite Obama's insurgency, the two parties maintained their traditional control of electoral politics. They fought each other tooth and nail on policy, but when it came to resisting a third choice, they stood shoulder to shoulder. A group called Unity08 (the predecessor of Americans Elect) proposed to nominate a candidate for president in 2008 via an Internet nominating convention. The group itself would not be supporting a particular candidate or a specific set of issues, but would offer voters an alternative by getting whoever won the online convention onto the presidential ballot in all fifty states. The Federal Election Commission, a creature of both parties, ruled in 2007 that Unity08 was subject to the campaign contribution limitations that allowed donors to give no more than five thousand dollars each. Unity08 then filed a lawsuit claiming that it was not a party but a nominating process. In July 2008, a federal judge ruled in favor of the FEC. Unity08 appealed the ruling, and on March 2, 2010, the appeals court reversed it, declaring that Unity08 was indeed a process and not a party and therefore could be financed by one person or many, contributing as much as they wanted, in order to give the electorate an alternative candidate to the Democrat and the Republican. When the FEC declined to appeal to the Supreme Court, that ruling became the law of the land, and Unity08 changed its name to Americans Elect.

Neither major party appears to have fully registered the implication of what happened. As late as the spring of 2011, Karl Rove, George W. Bush's former political guru, was saying that there would never be another third candidate in a presidential election.[7]

While each party was preparing for 2012 in the traditional way, Americans Elect was busy developing their alternative nominating process. Both parties suffered from the arrogance and laziness of a duopoly—think IBM and its mainframe before the arrival of the personal computer. The media was equally clueless, buying into the view, fostered by both parties, that the current system would never change. We seemed stuck with a few small states—Iowa, New Hampshire, South Carolina—arrogating to themselves the job of selecting who would get on the fall ballot. (In the 2012 Iowa Republican caucuses, fewer than 120,000 thousand voters participated.) The nomination process was hardly democratic. Nothing would change. Both parties liked it that way: If the selection process could be kept closed, there was big money at stake. One of the two parties would control the federal purse strings and reward its supporters; the other would have to be satisfied with the crumbs until the next election. No one could possibly emerge who could shake up the system.

Until now. Americans Elect was on the ballot in fifteen states by January 1, 2012, and had gathered the needed signatures in fifteen more states by the same date. By summer, Americans Elect hopes to have all fifty states covered. For the first time in our country's history, there will be an electoral process free of control by the major parties. The sign-up rate of citizens on petitions to get Americans Elect on the ballot in various states has been an astonishing 70 percent of those asked and includes nearly three million Americans.

The nominating process is simple. Citizens who are registered voters go online to www.americanselect.org and sign up as delegates. They are asked to suggest questions they want candidates to answer and make a contribution; both requests are optional. In mid-April 2012, the Americans Elect online convention begins. In a series of three preliminary votes, the field of candidates proposed by delegates will be narrowed to six by the end of May. At that point, each candidate must declare whether he or she will run and fill out an extensive candidate questionnaire that reflects the questions the delegates have posted and those that a bipartisan platform committee has chosen. In addition, the candidates must select a vice-presidential running mate "from a party other than their own" or someone who is an independent.[8] Between May 8 and June 1 there will be three weeks of debate among the six candidates (inevitably, these encounters will be televised) and then a secure online vote of all delegates to the Internet convention. If one of the six receives a majority, he or she will become the nominee. If not, the bottom three vote-getters must drop out. There will be a week of debate among the three remaining candidates. On June 8, there is another vote of delegates with the bottom candidate dropping out if there is still no majority. After two weeks of debate among the remaining two candidates, a winner will be determined by a vote on June 21. The nominee will then take his or her place on the ballot in potentially all fifty states on November 6.

The identity of the eventual nominee depends on who shows up as delegates. Will it be trade union members or Tea Party true believers? Will it be young people or older Americans? Will it be city dwellers or small-town activists? If a liberal or a moderate gets the nomination and ballot position, President Obama's re-election chances will be hurt. If a Tea Party candidate wins, the Republican nominee will be at a disadvantage. If lightning strikes and the Americans Elect candidate is the right person at the right time with the right set of views and communication skills, he or she could be elected president of the United States. No one knows how it will turn out. Obama partisans could vote for Republicans and vice versa. Mischief, even disaster, is possible—and so is political transformation.

What is so exciting about Americans Elect is that once again there is innovation in our democracy. Just as occurred in the expansion of the franchise and ensuring direct election of U.S. senators, Americans Elect takes the decision about who will appear on the ballot away from the exclusive control of the current political parties and gives it to citizens.

The Americans Elect process of 2012 could lead to a surprising development in 2014, when only the Congress stands for re-election. The court decision that allowed the financing of a presidential election process apart from the campaign finance laws also applies to an Americans Elect process in various congressional districts. Thus there is a real possibility that a third party could organize on the Americans Elect platform.

When third parties have emerged in the immediate past, they have always been centered around a candidate (Wallace, Anderson, Perot, Nader) and an office (the presidency). But the problem of our democracy is not the presidency, it is the Congress. Recall that the Congress had an approval rating of 6 percent last fall, whereas President Obama had a 40 percent rating. That tells me that Congress is more vulnerable to a third party effort than is the presidency. Even if an Americans Elect candidate won the White House in 2012, he or she would still have to deal with a Congress composed of Democrats and Republicans, whose joint purpose, if recent history is our

guide, would be to thwart the presidential agenda. Although the election of an Americans Elect president in 2012 is unlikely, the experience gained from the journey could be valuable in 2014.

There never has been a congressional third party. Today, that is the
opportunity. Other countries have several parties. Canada has five.
Germany, England, Japan, and Mexico have three major parties.
Granted, they are parliamentary democracies, but the New American
Party (let's call it) could learn from them. A congressional third party
whose objective would be the three R's—Raise our standard of living,
Reset our foreign policy, and Reform our politics—could have broad
appeal. Those who sought the party's nominations would be problem
solvers. Some might have political experience; others might not. Each
House candidate would be asked to commit to running for two additional terms if initially successful, and each Senate candidate would
be asked to commit to one term. The slogan could be "Six years for
the country." The party could field candidates in fifty congressional
districts and five senatorial elections. The objective would be to win
enough seats so that the party could be the fulcrum of power. If neither party had control, each would need the support of the brand-
new congressional party on one issue or another. In order to obtain
the New American Party's support, the major party seeking it would
have to make commitments to the agenda of the new party. This
leverage, combined with the clarity of a limited substantive program
articulated by its members, just might be the antidote to our partisan
paralysis and the catalyst to meet our country's needs.

No one knows how the Americans Elect process—or, for that
matter, the possible development of a third congressional party—
will turn out. When James Madison headed north from Virginia and
John Adams headed south from Massachusetts, each on his way to
Philadelphia for the Constitutional Convention in 1787, neither of
them knew how that would turn out, either. They knew that they

were dedicated to building a new country, one unlike any that had ever existed before. They were good people, honorable men, patriots who understood the stakes. They acted without cynicism, and with a deep-rooted belief in America's future. Why should we not assume that good and honorable people will show up at the Internet nominating convention? Why should we not expect that people who are currently uninvolved in politics will become involved in a congressional third party when they see what is possible? Why should we not expect that many of those who give to others with no thought of return will take up their responsibility as citizens and make their voices heard? The country needs all of us in order to face its future with confidence. Once again in American history, democratic innovation might herald a better day.

10

The Path to Renewal

A friend of mine who just came back from China told me that the one theme in all of her meetings there was the observation that the United States is in decline. These iterations were not a matter of Chinese bravado but only a description of what the Chinese perceived to be the facts. Our situation seems evident not only to the Chinese and other foreigners but also to millions of Americans— and too many of our citizens are losing hope. Hopelessness is a serious danger for a culture whose historical attitude has been optimism. It is the equivalent today of what fear was in the Great Depression. But, in the spirit of FDR when he confronted a fearful nation, I would say to those who feel the ground falling away under their feet that the only thing that can make our situation hopeless is hopelessness itself. It's time, in FDR's words, "to convert retreat into advance."

It is within our power to take control of our American future. The way forward is clear. To raise living standards, we must tax labor less and things more, adopt a massive infrastructure program, invest heavily in research, educate our citizens for a lifetime in a world of constant change, and reduce the structural budget deficit. To reset our foreign policy, we must recognize that while terrorism remains, the real threats rest in economic performance and strategic surprise and the challenge is to avoid lengthy military involvement in faraway lands while capitalizing on our real advantage: our example. Reforming our politics requires a constitutional amendment to limit the amount of money that can be spent in a political campaign, voluntary public financing of whatever amount is set by the Congress, and a plan to change the way congressional district lines are drawn. If we do all of this, our future will be bright.

None of these things can be accomplished without fortitude. Politicians should put country ahead of party and tell us the truth. We need brave leaders who are unafraid to take on the power of special interests, challenge the conventional Washington wisdom, and fight with all their energy for the emergence of a more creative and just society. The various Occupy protests this past winter against income inequality and the greed and mismanagement of the financial sector struck a chord with most Americans. Without our leaders explaining how, exactly, the country has arrived at this low point in its fortunes, the people's anger and desperation will continue undifferentiated. Without leaders who level with them about what needs to be done and how long it will take, there is no way to build support for the tough decisions necessary to solve our problems. People are tired of seeing the monied interests dominate the House of Representatives—the peoples' house. They're tired of narrow interests raiding the U.S. Treasury in collusion with congressmen who, when they leave office, are employed as lobbyists by the very industries whose interests they promoted in the Congress. (The same applies in spades to congressional staff.) They're tired of seeing their presidents appear at fund-raisers and hedge their bets and compromise their beliefs to raise campaign money. The people are tired of being taken for granted. They yearn for leaders who will level with them, not pander to them.

Leaders should begin by telling people where we are in comparison to other countries—and why, without action, we risk becoming a second-rate power. Too often, our politicians dismiss this kind of truth-telling as anti-American, whereas what's truly anti-American is a refusal to confront the cold, hard reality of our times. When Lincoln, in his second State of the Union address, spoke to a nation at war, he did not mince words:

> The dogmas of the quiet past are inadequate to the stormy present. The occasion is piled high with difficulty, and we must rise with the occasion. As our case is new, so we must think anew and act anew. We must disenthrall ourselves, and then we shall save our country.
>
> Fellow-citizens, we cannot escape history. We of this Congress and this Administration will be remembered in spite of ourselves. No personal significance or insignificance can spare one or another of us. The fiery trial through which we pass will light us down in honor or dishonor to the latest generation.

Today we need that same candor and sense of urgency. We need that same belief in our unique capacity to weather the storm and control our own destiny once again. We need to relinquish "the dogmas of the quiet past"—the imposition of reckless tax cuts, the promotion of income inequality, the surrender to international competitors, the denial of climate change and other environmental hazards, the objections to government's proper role in our lives. And we need to acknowledge the human costs of rapid technological change whose side effects—the loss of well-paying jobs, the need for re-education and portable health insurance—have not been effectively faced. The key is shared sacrifice now, so that all of us can have shared prosperity tomorrow—something we've missed out on for thirty years.

Our leaders should paint the picture of what we can become and how, once we tighten our belts for a while, our economy will improve. They should explain how we can revive the manufacturing sector, encourage innovation across the board, and invest for the long term. They should make the case for taxing work less and things more. They should describe the benefit to businesses of one national healthcare system. They should invest in education at all levels. They should show us how infrastructure investment can produce economic growth and jobs. They should talk about what it means to be American and what our historical values are. They should charge us to think anew, remind us of the goodness that lies within each of us, and inspire us with the courage they demonstrate by telling us the truth.

But energy flows not only from leaders to citizens but the other way as well. Above all, we need citizens who recognize their role in the American democracy. Our country has progressed because citizens wanted to change a national direction and decided to do something about it. From the abolitionists to the suffragettes to the civil-rights activists to the environmentalists, people have started movements that have shaped our larger politics. Their organized passions have changed our future.

In 2008, on that election night in Chicago, we made the mistake of believing that a leader can renew the country all by himself. But even someone who touched our hearts as deeply as Barack Obama cannot do it alone. A president can inspire and help to mobilize us, but then you need the lieutenants and sergeants who make the dream operational. Clarity from leaders is necessary but not sufficient. Only when it is joined with commitment from citizens can great things happen. Democracy is not a vicarious experience.

In our current circumstances, with the power of the Washington club never greater, only the people can free our government from its clutches and put our country on the path to renewal. In the internet age, apathy should not be an option. Citizens have to vote; for many, the vote is their most effective voice. But in order to vote wisely, citizens must take the time to become informed; otherwise the future will be hijacked by a combination of greed, self-indulgence, and excuse-making. The government will no longer belong to the people, and the people will suffer.

The Tea Party and Occupy Wall Street offer contrasting examples of citizen involvement. The Tea Party promulgated a very specific objective—Roll back government—and immediately converted its energy into electoral politics. The result was that in 2010 forty-three Tea Party Republicans won election to the Congress, and through their leverage in the Republican caucus they almost forced the country into bankruptcy during the debate on the debt limit in the summer of 2011. That's how quickly things can change. That's how easily the status quo can crumble. Occupy, on the other hand, while full of passion and solidarity, and even armed with a catchy slogan—"We're the 99 percent"—failed to have much of an impact on policy, because it had no specific objective. Some people argued that it was enough simply to point out inequality; a detailed program would have divided the movement. I say, better than an emotional movement that hesitates to develop a specific program would be a specific program—such as getting money out of politics—that attracts emotion to it. Whether we like it or not, passion only goes part way. Remember Martin Luther King Jr. and LBJ. It took both of them, working together as they did, to transform America in the 1960s.

So how do these thoughts reflect on 2012? To begin, citizens should insist on a presidential campaign about the future, not a blamefest about the past. The candidates should tell us specifically what they would do to raise our standard of living, reset our foreign policy, and reform our politics. Their narratives can have a historical dimension about how we got to where we are, but the bulk of their story must be about the future. If what you hear is only blame or bromides, change the channel. Haven't we had enough of those two things over the last twelve years?

Now is the time for citizens to insist on answers to real questions and for the media to serve the public more diligently than they serve their advertisers. Now is the time for follow-up questions and enough airtime for candidates to lay out their programs. What specifically will they do about jobs, the deficit, political corruption? How do they see America's role in the world? Now is the time for politicians to show us that they are more interested in doing something than in being somebody. There is a great difference between a genuine leader and a celebrity. The nation has had enough of politicians fascinated with celebrity. What we need are courageous leaders who serve the public and not themselves, who devise a plan to save the country and fight for it because they know that the well-being of millions of Americans is at stake.

My grandfather was an immigrant from Germany. On hot summer evenings, he would sit on his front porch in our small town with a bottle of Budweiser in hand, a Zane Grey novel on the table next to him, and the radio tuned to his first love, the St. Louis Cardinals, and tell his only grandson, me, what America meant to him. He said that America was great because it was free and because people seemed to care about each other. At our very best, throughout our history, that has been true. It's time to reclaim the legacy that reflects our best selves. It's time to elevate "What can we do for each other?" to the pedestal that for too long has been occupied by "What can I do for myself?"

The time for cooperation has arrived. No one person can fix the economy alone, much less the global financial system. No one alone can secure our national safety at home and abroad. No one person can protect our natural heritage or reduce global warming. No one person or group of self-made men can "raise all boats." Each of us has our individual part, but it will take all of us acting together to make America better.

In our current crisis, we must look for solutions from all directions. The richest man may not be the wisest. Wisdom is where you find it. On the individual and local level, solutions can come from a union hall or a community meeting or a parish church. They can come from a cab driver, a garbage collector, a shoeshine man in Pittsburgh, a welcome lady in Phoenix, a Walgreens executive in South Carolina, a public-health nurse in the Aleutian Islands, a professor at the University of Oklahoma. But solutions must also come from all of us working together at the national level to promote the general welfare.

Wisdom acts for the long term. It recognizes our human frailties, even as it celebrates our achievement. It knows that good and evil live in the same heart. It reminds us that we are our brother's keepers. It tells us that our great country needs to be revived and that its citizenry deep down wants to reclaim American democracy from the stranglehold of money and ideology. And it has faith in those citizens to succeed in that difficult task. Wisdom tells us that love is our truest impulse, that love translated into policy is justice, that we're all on this planet together, connected by our common humanity and hope for the future. Today what we need, above all, is that wisdom.

Acknowledgments

In writing this book, I owe much to others.

I want to thank my editors: Sara Lippincott, whose attention to both large themes and small details raised the quality of the book by several levels, and whose good humor made working together a pleasure; Betty Sue Flowers, whose counsel and wise observations challenged me at every step of the writing process, and whose steadfast support I treasure.

I thank my former wife, Ernestine Bradley, for her careful reading, knowledgeable insights, and helpful candor; and I thank our wonderful daughter, Theresa Anne Bradley, whose comprehensive comments and editorial suggestions are reflected throughout the book.

I thank my friends who read all or part of the book and made helpful suggestions: Herbert Allen III, Marcia Aronoff, Zoe Baird, David Booth, Terry Bracy, John Gearen, Scott Greenstein, Matt Henshon, Mellody Hobson, Devorah Klahr, Sandy Levinson, Jim

Manzi, Jessica Mathews, Daniel Okimoto, Don Roth, Barry Schuler, Shirley Tilghman, John Thornton, and Rick Wright.

I thank my assistant, Claire Falkner, who turned my scribble into clean text again and again and again, and whose considerable research skills improved the project. I also thank my longtime personal assistant, Beth Montgomery.

I thank my fact-checkers, Boris Fishman and Rob Liguori, whose thoroughness gave me great comfort.

I thank my agent, Art Klebanoff, who encouraged me and stood by me every step of the way.

Finally, I thank Allen & Co. for giving me the time to write the book.

Notes

Chapter 2

1. Susan Page, "Surveys Show an America That's Bruised, But Still Optimistic," USAToday online, Feb. 16, 2010, accessed at http://www .usatoday.com/news/nation/2010-02-16-optimistic-decade-americans _N.htm.

Chapter 3

1. Jill Schlesinger, "November Unemployment: Why the Big Drop?" Marketplace Economy, Dec, 2, 2011, accessed at http://www.marketplace .org/topics/economy/november-unemployment-why-big-drop.

2. "Dollars & Sense," *The Mark*, November 2011, volume 23, no. 11, 2–3.

3. "Public Priorities: Deficit Rising, Terrorism Slipping," Pew Research Center online, January 23, 2012, accessed at http://www.people-press.org /2012/01/23/public-priorities-deficit-rising-terrorism-slipping.

4. Census Bureau, March 17, 2011, accessed at http://www.census.gov /construction/nrc/historical_data.

5. Shaila Dewan and Louise Story, "U.S. May Back Refinance Plan for Mortgages," *New York Times*, August 24, 2011.

6. Bill Bradley, Tom Ridge, and David Walker, *Road to Recovery: Transforming America's Transportation* (Washington, DC: Carnegie Endowment for International Peace, 2011), accessed at http://carnegieendowment.org /2011/07/11/road-to-recovery-transforming-america-s-transportation /3e1h.

7. I co-chaired the committee, along with former Pennsylvania Governor and Secretary of Homeland Security Tom Ridge and former U.S. Comptroller General David Walker.

8. Bradley, Ridge, and Walker, *Road to Recovery*.

9. Michael Korda, *Ike: An American Hero* (New York: HarperCollins, 2007), p. 693; and David A. Nichols, *Eisenhower 1956* (New York: Simon & Schuster, 2011), 251, 264, 272–274.

10. Thilo Hanemann and Daniel H. Rosen, *An American Open Door? Maximizing the Benefits of Chinese Foreign Direct Investment*, Asia Society, May 2011, 9.

11. "The Budget and Economic Outlook: Fiscal Years 2011 to 2021," Congressional Budget Office, accessed at http://www.cbo.gov/ftpdocs /120xx/doc12039/01-26_FY2011Outlook.pdf, p. 166, Appendix B.

12. Ibid.: Total budget for 2015 is in Table 1-2, under Outlays. Total Outlays is 3.26T, with another 728BN off-budget. Total is 3.988T; Debt service is under "net interest" in Table 1-2: 336BN; Entitlements are in Table 1-4. Social Security is 897BN, Medicare is 662BN, and Medicaid 364BN; Defense is in Table 1-5: 756BN; The math: Outlays of 3.015T. That's 92.5% of 3.26T, and 75.6% of 3.988T.

13. "2010 Annual Report of the Boards of Trustees of the Federal Hospital Insurance and Federal Supplementary Medical Insurance Trust Funds," accessed at http://www.cms.gov/ReportsTrustFunds/downloads/tr2010.pdf.

14. "Letter to Ryan," accessed at http://www.cbo.gov/ftpdocs/92xx /doc9216/05-19-LongtermBudget_Letter-to-Ryan.pdf.

15. "The Feeblest Branch," *The Economist*, October 1, 2011.

16. *Nightly Business Report*, PBS, July 14, 2011.

17. See, for example, Professor J. Rufus Fears's lectures for the Teaching Company, *Famous Romans; The World was Never the Same: Events that Changed History; American Voices, interview with Bill Bradley*, February 26, 2012.

Chapter 4

1. "U.S. Election Will Cost $5.3 Billion, Center for Responsive Politics Predicts," OpenSecrets blog, Oct. 22, 2008, accessed at http://www.open secrets.org/news/2008/10/us-election-will-cost-53-billi.html.

2. "Most Members of Congress Enjoy Robust Financial Status, Despite Nation's Sluggish Economic Recovery," OpenSecrets blog, Nov. 15, 2011, accessed at http://www.opensecrets.org/news/2011/11/congress-enjoys -robust-financial-status.html.

3. "Chart of the Day: 9% of Americans Are Millionaires in 2011," *The* Atlantic online, May 5, 2011, accessed at http://www.theatlantic.com /business/archive/2011/05/chart-of-the-day-9-of-americans-are-million aires-in-2011/238458/#.

4. "Lobbying Database," OpenSecrets blog, accessed at http://www .opensecrets.org/lobby.

5. Mancur Olson, *The Rise and Decline of Nations* (New Haven, CT: Yale University Press, 1982).

6. "Lobbying Database," OpenSecrets blog.

7. "Interest Groups," OpenSecrets blog, accessed at http://www.open secrets.org/industries/index.php.

8. Gretchen Morgenson, *Reckless Endangerment: How Outsized Ambition, Greed, and Corruption Led to Economic Armageddon* (New York: Times Books, 2011), p. 19.

9. "FPA Statesman Dinner," Foreign Policy Association, Dec. 6, 2011, accessed at http://www.fpa.org/ckfinder/userfiles/files/Statesman%20Dinner _Kaufman_2011.pdf, p. 5.

10. Dan Burrows, "Chuck Prince, Former Citigroup CEO, Says He's Sorry," dailyfinance.com, April 8, 2010.

11. From a lecture by Warren Buffett in spring 1991 at Notre Dame. See http://www.tilsonfunds.com/BuffettNotreDame.pdf.

12. From "Citi Chief on Buyouts: 'We're Still Dancing,'" *New York Times* Dealbook, July 10, 2007.

13. "The Martin Era," *Time*, February 2, 1970.

14. Henry Kaufman, "Irresponsible Financial Behavior," remarks delivered before the Carnegie Council, New York City, June 20, 2011.

Chapter 5

1. Yochai Benkler, *The Penguin and the Leviathan: How Cooperation Triumphs over Self-Interest* (New York: Crown, 2011), 246.

2. Bill Drayton, "Collaborative Entrepreneurship," accessed at http://www.ashoka.org/sites/ashoka/files/Innovations_Collab_Ent_with_Empathy_Overview.pdf.

Chapter 6

1. Sabrina Tavernise, "Soaring Poverty Casts Spotlight on 'Lost Decade,'" *New York Times*, Sept. 13, 2010.

2. Robert B. Reich, "The Limping Middle Class," *New York Times*, Sept. 3, 2011.

3. U.S. Department of Health and Human Services Poverty Guidelines, January 2011.

4. "Income, Poverty and Health Insurance Coverage in the United States: 2010," U.S. Census Bureau, Sept. 13, 2011, accessed at http://www.census.gov/newsroom/releases/archives/income_wealth/cb11-157.html.

5. Quoted in Edward Luce, "The Crisis of Middle Class America," FT.Com/FT Magazine, July 30, 2010.

6. "Median and Average Sales Prices of New Homes Sold in United States," U.S. Census Bureau, accessed at http://www.census.gov/const/uspricemon.pdf.

7. Les Christie, "30% of Mortgages Are Underwater," CNNMoney.com, Feb. 9, 2011, accessed at http://money.cnn.com/2011/02/09/real_estate/underwater_mortgages_rising/index.htm; and Dan Levy, "U.S. Underwater

Mortgages May Reach 30%, Zillow Says," Bloomberg online, Aug. 11, 2009, accessed at http://www.bloomberg.com/apps/news?pid=newsarchive&sid =arpJHI9U42Rs.

8. Adrian Sainz, "Economy, Households, Banks Feel Drag from Pullback on Home-Equity Loans," *Seattle* Times, Dec. 25, 2009, accessed at http://seattletimes.nwsource.com/html/businesstechnology/2010598093 _homeequity26.html.

9. Mark Perry, "Manufacturing Jobs Drop to Lowest Level Since 1941, Below 9% of Workforce for the First Time," DailyMarkets.com, Aug. 21, 2009, accessed at http://www.dailymarkets.com/economy/2009/08/20 /manufacturing-jobs-drop-to-lowest-level-since-1941-below-9-of-work force-for-the-first-time.

10. Richard McCormack, "The Plight of American Manufacturing," *American Prospect*, December 21, 2009.-

11. E-mail on Dec. 7, 20011, from Hal Sirkin, coauthor of "Made in America, Again," The Boston Consulting Group, August 2011.

12. Department of Labor, Bureau of Labor Statistics, "Current Employment Statistics, December 2011."

13. Federal Reserve Board, "G.17 Statistics Release: Industrial Production and Capacity Utilization."

14. See http://money.cnn.com/2010/05/06/news/international/china _america.fortuneindex.htm.

15. James K. Jackson, "Foreign Investment, CFIUS, and Homeland Security: An Overview," Foreign Press Centers, Nov. 5, 2009, accessed at http://fpc.state.gov/documents/organization/133876.pdf, p. 4.

16. United Nations Conference on Trade & Development (UNCTAD), World Development Report, Annex Table 01.

17. Jon Gertner, "Does America Need Manufacturing," *New York Times*, August 24, 2011.

18. Susan Hockfield, "Manufacturing a Recovery," *New York Times*, August 29, 2011.

19. Ibid.

20. J. Bradford Jensen, *Global Trade in Services: Fear, Facts and Offshoring* (Washington, DC: Peterson Institute for International Economics, 2011).

21. Peter Mott, "Single-Payer Health System Could Save Billions," Physicians for a National Health Program, Dec. 7, 2008, accessed at http://www.pnhp.org/news/2008/december/singlepayer_health_.php; and Bernie Sanders, "Health Care," Feb. 11, 2012, accessed at http://sanders .senate.gov/legislation/issue/?id=a5823331-b1c8-46a1-864f-a5986cf 82a9b.

22. Bill Drayton, "Hire People, Retire Things," What Matters, July 19, 2011, accessed at http://whatmatters.mckinseydigital.com.

23. Ibid.

24. June Taylor, Phil Heinrich, et al., "Job Creation Tax Options, Summary," Get America Working, Dec. 1, 2011, accessed at http://www.get americaworking.org/node/21.

25. E-mails from Steve Kent and June Thomas, Get America Working!, Jan. 4, 2012.

Chapter 7

1. James MacGregor Burns, The Workshop of Democracy (New York: Knopf, 1985), 543.

2. "The Great Depression," History.com, accessed at http://www .history.com/topics/great-depression.

3. Jean Edward Smith, FDR (New York: Random House, 2008), 289.

4. Ibid.

5. David R. Francis, "Supply-siders Take Some Lumps," Christian Science Monitor, October 1, 2007.

6. George Lakoff, "Why Democracy Is Public: The American Dream Beats the Nightmare," HuffingtonPost, July 28, 2011, accessed at http:// www.huffingtonpost.com/george-lakoff/why-democracy-is-public-t_b _911205.html.

Chapter 8

1. John M. Barry, The Great Influenza (Penguin, 2004), 302.

2. George Kennan, American Diplomacy 1900–1950 (IL: University of Chicago Press, 1951), 69.

3. Joseph Nye, "Optimistic or Pessimistic About America," *Commentary Magazine*, Oct. 30, 2011, accessed at http://www.commentarymagazine.com /2011/10/30/optimistic-or-pessimistic-about-america-joseph-nye

4. Brady E. Hamilton, Joyce A. Martin, and Stephanie J. Ventura, "Births: Preliminary Data for 2010," Centers for Disease Control and Prevention, accessed at http://www.cdc.gov/nchs/data/nvsr/nvsr60/nvsr60 _02.pdf, page 4; and George Friedman, *The Next Hundred Years* (New York: Anchor Books, 2010), 53–54.

5. Rickety, "2010 Defense Spending by Country," Rickety blog, June 4, 2011, accessed at http://www.rickety.us/2011/06/2010-defense-spending -by-country.

6. William Overholt, personal e-mail that reflects the central theme of his 2008 book, *Asia, America and the Transformation of Geopolitics* (New York: Cambridge University Press, 2007).

7. Clay Dillow, "In 2020, Take a High-Speed Train from Beijing to London," *Popular* Science, March 16, 2010, accessed at http://www.popsci.com /science/article/2010-03/china-plans-beijing-london-high-speed-rail-link.

8. Michael Heath and Jason Scott, "Australia Boom Means Men Without Degree Earn More Than Bernanke," Bloomberg online, April 1, 2011, accessed at http://www.bloomberg.com/news/2011-04-01/australia-boom -means-men-without-degree-earn-more-than-bernanke.html.

9. "FIFO, FIFO; It's Off to Work We Go," Flights Australia blog, Sept. 22, 2011, accessed at http://www.flightsaustralia.com.au/blog/?p=11.

10. David Caploe, "China High-End Value added—the German Connection," economywatch.com, September 14, 2010; and "VDMA Steps Up Fight Against Product Piracy," accessed at http://www.vdma.org /wps/portal/Home/en/Branchen/P/KUG/Presse/kug_A_20100526_VDMA _fight_against_product_piracy_en?WCM_GLOBAL_CONTEXT=/vdma /Home/en/Branchen/P/KUG/Presse/kug_A_20100526_VDMA_fight _against_product_piracy_en.

11. Daniel Schäfer, "Chinese Push into Germany's Heart and Soul," *Financial Times*, October 11, 2010.

12. Kishore Mahbubani, "Smart Power, Chinese Style," The American Interest, March/April 2008, accessed at http://www.the-american-interest .com/article-bd.cfm?piece=406.

13. Personal communication from William H. Overholt; about his multiple conversations with Chinese diplomats, academics, and generals, including General Pan of China Reform Forum, the Think Tank of the Central Party School of the Chinese Communist Party.

14. Joel Brenner, *America the Vulnerable: Inside the New Threat Matrix of Digital Espionage, Crime and Warfare* (New York: Penguin Press, 2011), p. 118.

15. William H. Overholt, "Awaiting Xi Jinping: The New China," *Washington Quarterly Review,* March 2012; and Chas Freeman (Ambassador and USFS, Ret.), speech at China Maritime Institute, Naval War College, Newport, Rhode Island, May 10, 2011.

Chapter 9

1. Wallace Stegner, *Beyond the Hundredth Meridian: John Wesley Powell and the Second Opening of the West* (New York: Houghton Mifflin, 1954), 304.

2. The American Promise, March 15, 1965; and also *Public Papers of the Presidents of the United States: Lyndon Johnson, 1965* (Government Printing Office, 1966), Vol. 1, entry 107, 281–287.

3. Paul Krugman, "The Conscience of a Liberal," *New York Times,* July 28, 2009.

4. "2012 Competitive House Race Chart," Cook Political Report, Jan. 26, 2012, and updated Feb. 9, 2012, accessed at http://cookpolitical.com /charts/house/competitive.php.

5. George Lakoff, *Thinking Points: Communicating Our American Values and Vision* (Farrar, Straus, and Giroux, 2006), see generally Chapter 2, "Biconceptualism"; see also http://www.cognitivepolicyworks.com/resource -center/thinking-points.

6. "2004 Servey of Consumer Finances: Summary Results," Federal Reserve, accessed at http://www.federalreserve.gov/econresdata/scf/scf _2004.htm. An easier-to-digest form of the data is found in Alice H. Munnell and Steven A. Sass, *Working Longer: The Solution to the Retirement Income Challenge* (Washington, DC: Brookings Institution Press, 2009), 5.

7. Jim Meyers and Kathleen Walter, "Rove: There Won't Be a Third-Party Candidate," Newsmax, Nov. 29, 2011, accessed at http://www.news max.com/Newsfront/Rove-Third-Party-Candidate/2011/11/28/id/419316.

8. Most of the Americans Elect information can be found through the AE Briefing Book, which is available on the AE website, http://static .americanselect.org/sites/files/official-documents/AE%20Candidate %20Book%2011.pdf; see also http://static.americanselect.org/sites/files /official-documents/AE%20ONE%20SHEET.pdf; see also AE's draft rules for potential candidates at http://static.americanselect.org/sites/files/official -documents/Draft%209-30-11%20Rules.pdf; see also general nominating information at http://www.americanselect.org/official-documents.

Suggested Reading on America

Adams, Henry. *History of the United States of America During the Administrations of Thomas Jefferson.*

————. *History of the United States of America During the Second Administration of Thomas Jefferson, 1805–1809, Volume 2.*

Allen, Frederick Lewis. *Only Yesterday: An Informal History of the 1920s.*

Boorstin, Daniel J. *The Image: A Guide to Pseudo-Events in America.*

Branch, Taylor. *Parting the Waters: America in the King Years 1954–1963.*

Brown, Dee Alexander. *Bury My Heart at Wounded Knee: An Indian History of the American West.*

Burns, James MacGregor. *The Vineyard of Liberty: The American Experiment, Volume 1.*

————. *The Workshop of Democracy: The American Experiment, Volume 2.*

————. *Crossroads of Freedom: The American Experiment, Volume 3.*

Caro, Robert A. *The Path to Power (The Years of Lyndon Johnson, Volume 1).*

————. *Means of Ascent (The Years of Lyndon Johnson, Volume 2).*

————. *Master of the Senate (The Years of Lyndon Johnson, Volume 3).*

Chace, James. *1912: Wilson, Roosevelt, Taft and Debs—The Election that Changed the Country.*

Chernow, Ron. *The House of Morgan: An American Banking Dynasty and the Rise of Modern Finance.*

Coles, Robert. *The Call of Stories: Teaching and the Moral Imagination.*

Crunden, Robert Morse. *Ministers of Reform: The Progressives' Achievement in American Civilization, 1889–1920.*

DeTocqueville, Alexis. *Democracy in America, Volumes I and II.*

Dreiser, Theodore. *An American Tragedy.*

Eisenhower, Dwight. *Eisenhower's Farewell Address to the Nation.*

Emerson, Ralph Waldo. *Self Reliance.*

Engler, Robert. *Brotherhood of Oil: Energy Policy and the Public Interest.*

Fiedler, Leslie A. *Love and Death in the American Novel.*

Fischer, David Hackett. *Albion's Seed: Four British Folkways in America* (America: A Cultural History).

Fitzgerald, F. Scott. *The Great Gatsby.*

Galbraith, John Kenneth. *The Great Crash 1929.*

Goodwin, Doris Kearns. *Team of Rivals.*

Greenstein, Fred I. *The Hidden-Hand Presidency: Eisenhower as Leader.*

Heilbroner, Robert L. *The Worldly Philosophers: The Lives, Times and Ideas of the Great Economic Thinkers.*

Hofstadter, Richard. *The Age of Reform.*

Jay, John, Alexander Hamilton, and James Madison. *The Federalist Papers.*

Jensen, Richard J., William H. Lyon, Philip Reed rulon, eds. *Great Speehes in American History.*

Kean, Thomas H. and Lee Hamilton. *The 9/11 Commission Report: Final Report of the National Commission on Terrorist Attacks Upon the United States.*

Kennan, George F. *American Diplomacy.*

Kindleberger, Charles P. *Manias, Panics, and Crashes: A History of Financial Crises.*

Korda, Michael. *Ike: An American Hero.*

Lewis, Michael. *The New New Thing: A Silicon Valley Story.*

Limerick, Patricia Nelson. *The Legacy of Conquest: The Unbroken Past of the American West.*

Link, Arthur Stanley. *Woodrow Wilson: Revolution, War, and Peace.*

————. *Woodrow Wilson and the Progressive Era.*

———. *Wilson*.

Malcolm X. *The Autobiography of Malcolm X*.

Maclean, Norman. *A River Runs Through It*.

McCullough, David G. *John Adams*.

———. *Truman*.

McMurtry, Larry. *Lonesome Dove: A Novel*.

McPhee, John. *Coming into the Country*.

———. *The Curve of Binding Energy: A Journey into the Awesome and Alarming World of Theodore B. Taylor*.

———. *Uncommon Carriers*.

McPherson, Harry. *A Political Education: A Washington Memoir*.

McPherson, James M. *Battle Cry of Freedom: The Civil War Era* (Oxford History of the United States).

Melville, Herman. *Moby Dick*.

Miller, Arthur. *Death of a Salesman*.

Miller, Merle. *Plain Speaking: An Oral Biography of Harry S. Truman*.

Mitford, Jessica. *American Way of Death*.

Morgan, Ted. *FDR: A Biography*.

Morgenson, Gretchen. *Reckless Endangerment: How Outsized Ambition, Greed, and Corruption Led to Economic Armageddon*.

Morrison, Toni. *Beloved*.

Nichols, John Treadwell. *The Milagro Beanfield War*.

Okimoto, Daniel I. *American in Disguise*

Schlesinger, Arthur Meier. *The Age of Jackson*.

———. *The Cycles of American History*.

Sherwood, Robert E. *Roosevelt and Hopkins: An Intimate History*.

Smith, Jean Edward. *FDR*.

Sorensen, Theodore C. *Kennedy: The Classic Biography*.

Stegner, Wallace. *Beyond the Hundredth Meridian: John Wesley Powell and the Second Opening of the West*.

Steinbeck, John. *The Grapes of Wrath*.

Twain, Mark. *The Adventures of Huckleberry Finn*.

Updike, John. *Rabbit, Run*.

———. *Rabbit Is Rich*.

————. *Rabbit at Rest.*

U.S. Senate Committee on Banking and Currency. *The Pecora Report: The 1934 Report on the Practices of Stock Exchanges from the "Pecora Commission."*

Vidal, Gore. *Lincoln: A Novel* (American Chronicle Series).

Warren, Earl. *Report of the President's Commission on the Assassination of President Kennedy.*

Whitman, Walt. *The Complete Poems* (Penguin Classics).

Wills, Garry. *Nixon Agonistes: The Crisis of the Self-Made Man.*

Index